JEREMIAH HACKER

Jeremiah Hacker, 1801-1895

(Image from the Collections of Maine Historical Society;
reproduced with permission)

JEREMIAH HACKER

JOURNALIST, ANARCHIST, ABOLITIONIST

Rebecca M. Pritchard

Frayed Edge Press
Philadelphia, PA
2019

Copyright 2019

Published in 2019 by Frayed Edge Press

https://frayededgepress.com

Publishers Cataloging-in-Publication Data

Names: Pritchard, Rebecca M., author.
Title: Jeremiah Hacker : journalist, anarchist, abolitionist / Rebecca M. Pritchard
Description: Philadelphia, PA : Frayed Edge Press, 2019. | Includes 7 b&w illustrations. | Summary: Biography and overview of the writings of Jeremiah Hacker, editor of *The Pleasure Boat*, 19th C. Maine's most controversial newspaper. He worked to end slavery, poverty, and inequality of women. He advocated for land reform and prison reform, and broke with all organized religion. His most controversial position was for peace prior to the Civil War.
Identifiers: LCCN 2018939686 | ISBN 9781642510065 (softcover) | ISBN 9781642510072 (ebook)
Subjects: LCSH: Hacker, Jeremiah, 1801-1895. | Journalists--Biography. | Maine--Portland--History--19th century. | New Jersey--History--19th century. | | BISAC: HISTORY / United States / 19th Century. | HISTORY / United States / State & Local / New England (CT, MA, ME, NH, RI, VT). | HISTORY / United States / State & Local / Middle Atlantic (DC, DE, MD, NJ, NY, PA).
Classification: LCC F25.P75 2018 (print) | LCC F25.P75 (ebook) | DDC 974.1--dc23
LC record available at https://lccn.loc.gov/2018939686

To Michael and Alison

Contents

List of Illustrations	ix
Acknowledgements	xi
Introduction: Promenade Deck	1

Part One: Biography

Chapter 1 - Early Influences: Farming and the Society of Friends	13
Chapter 2 - Early Pursuits: Teaching and Trading	19
Chapter 3 - "A Stranger, Among Strangers in Truth": Hacker the Missionary	25
Chapter 4 - *The Pleasure Boat* Captain	33
Chapter 5 - Running Aground: The Civil War, Spiritualism, and Hacker's Last Years in Portland	41
Chapter 6 - The Last Song of Jeremiah Hacker	49

Part Two: Writings

Part Two Introduction: Major Themes and Language Use in *The Pleasure Boat*	59

Chapter 7 - Reformers' Cabin: *The Pleasure Boat* as
Reform Journal   63

Chapter 8 - Free Land Office: Hacker on Land Reform   71

Chapter 9 - Pirates Cabin: Hacker on the Government   79

Chapter 10 - Church-Goer's Cabin: Hacker on Organized
Religion   85

Chapter 11 - Spiritualists' Cabin: Hacker on Women's
Rights   91

Chapter 12 - Humanity's Courtroom: Hacker on Juvenile
Justice   97

Chapter 13 - Conversation Room: Analysis of Hacker's
Ideas   107

Conclusion: Finding Hacker's Place in History   113

Bibliography   119

About the Author   129

Plates follow page 55

Illustrations

Plates following page 55

Frontispiece — Jeremiah Hacker portrait

Plate 1. — John Neal portrait

Plate 2. — First page of the first issue of *The Pleasure Boat*

Plate 3. — Drawing of Munjoy Hill

Plate 4. —Drawing of the Old Exchange

Plate 5. — Photograph of haying at the State School for Boys' Farm

Plate 6. — Jeremiah Hacker's grave

Acknowledgements

I would like to thank my professors at University of Southern Maine: Drs. Ardis Cameron, Joseph Conforti, Donna Cassidy, and Kent Ryden. You challenged me to go deeper into this subject than I would have on my own. You all were instrumental in helping me complete the master's thesis that became draft one of this book.

Thank you to the librarians and staff at Maine Historical Society. It was librarian William David Barry who first introduced me to *The Pleasure Boat* and its author, Jeremiah Hacker. Research librarians are like matchmakers. Bill knew my interests and reading habits well enough to know Mr. Hacker and I would get along just fine. Thanks also to Sofia Yalouris at Maine Historical, who helped obtain the images to bring this story to life.

While studying someone who almost nobody knew about, I felt a special kinship to the few people who did. To the handful of Hacker enthusiasts I have met along the way who have shared their knowledge, resources, observations, and even publishing information: thank you. These include Betsey Sheehan, Herb Adams, David Sachs, and Robert Helms. I also thank everyone who has read this book in its early stages. Besides those mentioned above, readers include Michael Pritchard, Jan Church, Elizabeth Koopman, Rosalie Tyler Paul, Theresa Hodgdon, and John and Ann McDonald. Thank you all for your time, your help, and your valuable input. A special thanks to my editor, Alison Lewis, for your guidance in turning this manuscript into a book. It's been an exciting process, and a pleasure to work with you.

Thanks to all my family for your love and support throughout this long process. This book would not be possible without encouragement from all of you. Mom and Dad – it really started with you encouraging me to write when I was very small. And finally, to my husband Michael and daughter Alison: you have allowed me the time I needed to lose myself in this project. You have gotten me through. To you this book is fondly dedicated.

Rebecca M. Prichard, 2018

Introduction: Promenade Deck

There was something unique about Jeremiah Hacker. A tall journalist who walked the same route every week through the seaside city of Portland, he was a highly visible figure around town in the middle years of the nineteenth century. Even from far away, people could tell who he was as he strode the dusty city streets. Perhaps it was his long, determined gait—like someone who was going out to spread "the Truth"—the focused, straightforward walk of someone who was not sidetracked by the noises around him. He was, in fact, deaf to all sounds except those directed straight at him, which he captured through an ear trumpet. He carried his trumpet and copies of his newspaper, *The Pleasure Boat*, wherever he went.

Jeremiah Hacker's name could not have fit him better had he chosen it himself. He was a Hacker by name, and a hacker by trade. That is, with his sharp pen and sharper wit, he hacked away at all that was wrong in the world. This was a pun he was fond of using himself. His first name, Jeremiah, was uncommonly fitting, too. An independent, deeply religious and somewhat cantankerous man, he wrote with a sense of urgency that rivaled the Old Testament prophets. Like his namesake of old, this nineteenth-century Jeremiah saw it as his mission "to root up and tear down, to destroy and demolish, to build and to plant."[1]

---

1. Jeremiah, 1:10. Donald Senior, ed., *The Catholic Study Bible: The New American Bible* (New York: Oxford University Press, 1990), 950.

Hacker's appearance was most unusual. His eyes were stern under thick eyebrows. His bushy beard flowed out over his patched coat, which he wore with perfect dignity. Hacker felt "required to clothe himself according to the plainness and simplicity of the truth."[2] He wore a hat described as "broad-brimmed," and a coat that a friend had given him. This was, in fact, the famous "old drab coat" which he mentioned every week in his newspaper. *The Pleasure Boat*, he said, was available "at the office... in the 'old drab coat.'" What he meant was that he had no office; or, rather, that he was his own traveling office. He wrote the newspaper on his knee each week at Cross Street Boarding House where he lived, and he paid a printer on Exchange Street to publish it. Subscribers could get the newspaper from "Uncle Samuel" (the postal service). Non-subscribers could buy the paper at Bearce's Periodicals or at Cross Street Boarding House, or from him directly as he made his rounds through the city in his old drab coat.[3]

Hacker could be seen walking through the business district, the rich neighborhoods, the tenements, and those parts of town that were not "respectable in the day time," but were "frequented by many of the respectable in the evening."[4] He was hailed by young boys on their mother's errands, by poor old men on crutches, by well-to-do ladies who would call and wave to him from their doorways. He stopped businessmen and ministers on the street, trying to interest them in buying a paper. He did not always meet with success, but neither did he give up easily, so eager was he to spread his message to those who needed to hear it. When one man refused a newspaper because it was "full of lies," Hacker insisted he take one anyway. He asked the man to "read it and mark all the falsehoods with a pen, and return it to me, so that I may be sensible of my errors."[5]

---

2. *The Pleasure Boat*, Nov. 13, 1847: 1.

3. *The Pleasure Boat*, Nov. 3, 1845: 1.

4. *The Pleasure Boat*, July 21, 1845: 3.

5. *The Pleasure Boat*, Aug. 4, 1845: 3.

Sometimes Hacker was sought out by those he had offended in a previous issue. When met with an angry reader, Hacker would hold his trumpet tightly against his ear "so that not a word should be lost" and he heard the complainant out patiently. As the cursing grew in volume, Hacker would say, "A little louder, I cannot hear you distinctly." Thus, he would wear out his foes.[6]

Hacker went down to the waterfront to spread his word among the sailors—the "almost friendless seamen" as he called them—for whom he had great respect. His brother had been a shipmaster and Hacker was a metaphorical sailor himself, as Captain of *The Pleasure Boat*. He gave copies of the *Boat* to sailors, not only to read for their own edification, but also to bring to other shores.[7]

He went into temperance shops and grog shops, selling his paper to teetotalers and drunkards alike. Though he advocated temperance in all things, including alcohol, he had better luck selling to the drunkards. One reader asked Hacker why his paper had "more patronage among the rum shops, the licentious and the rabble than any other part of the community." He answered that he wrote the paper "with the intention of spreading truth among such as need it most, and if publicans and sinners are willing to support truth, I know not by what authority any can forbid them." Reminding the reader that Jesus dined with sinners, Hacker continued, "If such truths as are contained in this sheet find more patronage among the rum shops, the licentious and the rabble are nearer the kingdom of heaven than the others...."[8]

Hacker went regularly into the county jail to spread his word among the prisoners: the men, women, and children who were awaiting trial or serving their sentences and were as hungry as anyone for what Hacker

---

6. Charles Holden, "The Origin and History of the Newspaper Press in Cumberland County." *Editors' and Publishers' Association of Maine, at Portland, August 4th & 5th, 1869* (Portland, ME: Monitor Printing, 1869), p. 43.

7. *The Pleasure Boat*, Nov. 24, 1845: 2.

8. *The Pleasure Boat*, Mar. 27, 1846: 3.

called "the Truth."[9] While there, he saw how the inmates were treated and used that as material for the *Boat*. He became an outspoken advocate for prison reform and was the first journalist in Portland to call for a separate facility for children, to focus on reform rather than punishment.

Hacker sought out blind men being led along by children and stopped in the homes of poor widows. "Mr. Hacker, if I had a cent in the world I would buy one of your papers," said one old man on the street, "I thank God that he has raised one up to plead for the poor and the needy."[10] If anyone wanted a *Boat* and couldn't pay for one, Hacker gave it for free. He encouraged the rich to pay more than the asking price of two cents so he could afford to be generous to the poor. Wherever he went he looked for new readers, new converts to his cause. Person by person, he tried to convert the whole city of Portland, the whole state of Maine, and beyond.

In between issues of the *Boat*, Hacker traveled far and wide. Because of his deafness, he was difficult to talk to and was known to be "somewhat cranky in his radicalism";[11] nonetheless, he was able to captivate people. While selling subscriptions in New York City, Hacker found a man who was willing to be an agent for *The Pleasure Boat*, "without any compensation or reward other than the satisfaction arising from the dissemination of truth." The agent, R.C. White, wrote to Hacker that his visit to the city had "given [White] more pleasure than the visit of the President of the United States."[12]

A correspondent to *The Voice of Industry*, a progressive workers' rights newspaper in Boston, wrote in to describe a visit he had with Hacker. He described the journalist as "a good man, possessing great benevolence and working hard among the poor and the despised." He recommended that readers of the *Industry* get to know both the journalist and his

---

9. Hacker called his own writing "the truth" quite often, often spelling it with a capital T, as in his statement, "There should be humanity enough in this city to support one little paper in favor of TRUTH." *The Pleasure Boat*, Apr. 1, 1845: 2.

10. *The Pleasure Boat*, Aug. 4, 1845: 2.

11. *Portland Transcript*, Sept. 11, 1895: 190.

12. *The Pleasure Boat*, July 17, 1847: 1.

newspaper: "Take the Pleasure Boat if you want to get plain truth, and if you ever go to Portland be sure to see friend Hacker. I hope all will follow his advice to me, 'Be good and do good.'"[13]

Once, Hacker went to a cattle show in Saccarappa, a neighborhood of Westbrook,[14] where he spent the day talking to farmers and selling the *Boat*. He sold eight annual subscriptions, a hundred individual papers, and then "threw a hundred or two into the air, which the wind scattered among the multitude, who caught most of them before they reached the ground"; Hacker left satisfied.[15] Like the farmer in the Bible, he had scattered his seeds of "the Truth" to take root, or not, on the fertile soil or the hardened earth.

Whether or not his ideas took root in his own time, Hacker has now been largely lost to history. The story of Jeremiah Hacker is the story of a New England radical, a man who devoted his life to spreading his ideas and changing people's hearts (thereby changing the world) through his writing. "He was a powerful man," wrote Hacker's contemporary, Charles Holden.[16] But as a simple journalist who disdained politics and distrusted what most people called progress, Hacker never made a name for himself in history. His writings, which have never been published in any form other than his four-page newspaper, remain in the back rooms of libraries to be rediscovered by students and historians. Why should history include the likes of Hacker? Why is he important? There are several answers to these questions.

Hacker deepens our understanding of New England history. He helps shift our focus northward to Portland, Maine, which was one of the many hotbeds of reform in the nineteenth century. Much has already been written about cities such as Boston, Massachusetts, and Rochester, New York, as centers of radical reform at this time. Portland, while it

---

13. *The Voice of Industry*, Oct. 29, 1847: 2.

14. George J. Varney, *A Gazetteer of the State of Maine* (Boston: B.B. Russell, 1886), p. 486. Saccarappa was its own village, complete with railroad station and post office, within the town of Westbrook.

15. *The Pleasure Boat*, Nov. 3, 1845: 3.

16. Holden, "Origin and History." 43.

gets overshadowed by these larger cities, was a leader in some areas. Portland reformers were forerunners in the temperance movement; they were heavily involved in abolition (with many Portland abolitionists participating in the Underground Railroad); and they championed the causes of women's rights, moral reform, aid to the poor, and peace. Out of this culture of reform, Hacker emerged as a genuine homegrown radical whose newspaper gave voice to many of the more revolutionary ideas that were floating around at the time.

As a historical document, *The Pleasure Boat* tells some fascinating stories. First, it tells us about the fever of reform that existed in the Portland region, as well as in the country at large. Hacker was a well-read and well-informed radical who traded with newspapers all over the country and wrote about national trends in reform. Too independent to ever endorse a cause completely, Hacker often criticized fellow reformers for not going far enough. For example, he criticized abolitionists for speaking out against slavery, while at the same time purchasing products produced by slave labor. He criticized peace activists for paying taxes to a government that engaged in warfare. Considering himself to be a lonely voice of reason above the rabble of popular reform movements, Hacker provided (and continues to provide) an interesting perspective on all reform movements of his time.

Second, *The Pleasure Boat* tells us about the city of Portland itself, between the years of 1845 and 1862. As a reformer, Hacker was interested in the common people and how their lives could be improved. To this end, he filled his newspaper with what we now consider "social history": descriptions of the poor and destitute, the young boys carrying buckets of pig-swill through the streets, the sailors, the free blacks, the immigrants, the orphaned children, the jail inmates, and all the many people who made up the fabric of the city of Portland, but who often have been overlooked by history books. The fact that Hacker wrote about such people in detail refocuses our own view of the past and helps us fill in some of the gaps in the traditional historical narrative. Keeping in mind that Hacker was not an objective narrator, it can be illuminating to examine his influences, and his goals for portraying Portland and its people in the ways that he did.

Finally, the newspaper tells us a lot about Hacker himself. Nineteenth-century newspapers were not what would be considered objective journalism and *The Pleasure Boat* was more opinionated than most. One learns a great deal about Hacker's own likes and dislikes, as well as his passions and beliefs. To a lesser extent, one also learns something about his personal life. As he portrays himself, Hacker was a disowned Quaker with strong religious convictions who disdained organized religion. He was from a large family in Brunswick and was close to his surviving brothers and sisters who lived throughout southern and central Maine. He had been orphaned "at a tender age" and began to lose his hearing as a teenager. In addition to his work as a journalist and publisher, Hacker was at various times an itinerant preacher, a subsistence farmer, and a family man. While he and his wife, Mittie, had no biological children, they adopted a daughter. All of these bits of information can be gleaned from the pages of *The Pleasure Boat*.

There is much, of course, that Hacker didn't write about himself, and mysteries abound about his personal life. What caused him to go deaf? Why did he and Mittie not have children? He wrote in the language of sailors, but did Hacker himself ever go to sea? The quest to know Jeremiah Hacker as a person becomes an interesting story in itself. Here is a man who spent his life writing, yet never became a significant part of written history. While he was an influential and even inspiring figure to many individuals involved in reform during his lifetime, he and his writings have been posthumously forgotten. Researching his life is a bit like researching an anonymous great-great-great-granduncle: you see snippets of him here and there—in this directory, in that census, in these letters. Putting the pieces together can assemble enough of a picture of this man to understand who he was in the context of his times, and to gain a new understanding of those times through his life and ideas.

This book is in two parts. Part One is a biography of Hacker and Part Two is an overview of his writings. Over the course of Hacker's long career, he wrote and edited three reform journals. The first one, *The Pleasure Boat*, lasted seventeen years. Hacker left an enormous body of written work, from which Part Two of this book attempts to extract the essence. Each of Hacker's favorite topics is given a chapter, and each chapter is named after a column in *The Pleasure Boat*. For example, when Hacker wrote about the government, he relegated this to the "Pirates' Cabin" of his *Boat*. His column headings were colorful and sometimes provided commentaries themselves.

What follows concerns the life and writings of Jeremiah Hacker, two topics worthy of re-discovery in our current time.

Part One:
Biography

Chapter 1

EARLY INFLUENCES: FARMING AND THE SOCIETY OF FRIENDS

Jeremiah Hacker was profoundly influenced by his early years in rural Brunswick. He knew farm life as a boy, and city life as a man, and he preferred the former to the latter. As a journalist, he advised his readers to leave the city and get some land on which to farm. He advised those readers who already lived in the country to stay put. He authored articles to educate his readers on farming matters, such as humane methods to keep crows away from the corn. Perhaps it was his own disappointment at having to leave his family's homestead after the death of his parents and make his living in the city that later made him such an outspoken advocate for land reform. Every man, he said, should have access to some land on which he could earn a living the natural way.

The story of Jeremiah Hacker, in this light, can be seen as the story of a man who struggled his whole life to get back to the earth and the pastoral life he loved. "Man was designed to till the earth,"[17] he wrote in *The Pleasure Boat*, and in his case, it was true. Hacker was born on a farm but had to spend most of his life in the city. Nonetheless, he was able to farm on small plots here and there in the outskirts of Portland, Maine—first on Mount Joy (currently Munjoy Hill), and then near Back Cove, where the land was poor and he barely scraped by. Eventually, he left the city behind and settled down as an old man in the farming community of Vineland, New Jersey, where he wrote contemplative

---

17. *The Pleasure Boat*, September 22, 1845: 4.

articles on agricultural topics and died peacefully at the ripe old age of ninety-four.

Between childhood and retirement, Hacker had another all-consuming passion: spreading his ideas. He did this first as a teacher, then as an itinerant preacher, and finally as the writer and publisher of a long-running Portland newspaper. The ideas he spread so passionately ranged from the religious (though some called them anti-religious) to the political, to the social. Through his preaching and his writing, he championed causes that were often unpopular but which he deemed necessary, such as the abolition of slavery, pacifism, the achievement of economic justice, and the end of government, prisons, and organized religion. But before we can understand Jeremiah Hacker as a writer and reformer, we must first try to understand him as a person.

Jeremiah Hacker was born in 1801 into a large Quaker family living on the western outskirts of Brunswick, Maine, a short distance from the Quaker meeting house in South Durham.[18] There is still a Quaker meeting house on that spot and the Hacker family name is immortalized nearby in "Hacker Road," a paved street that winds through the still-rural corner of Brunswick. Other than these two landmarks of Hacker's early life, not much information can be found about his childhood. Although so little is known about him personally at this stage of his life, looking at the community he grew up in may provide some insight.

"Quaker" was the unofficial term, at one time derogatory but later universally accepted, to denote members of the Religious Society of Friends.[19] Founded by George Fox in England in the mid-seventeenth

---

18. Hacker described a visit to his childhood home, which he made by traveling to South Durham by stage, during which he visited some Quaker friends there, and then "after a pleasant walk stood once more in Brunswick, on the spot where I was born...." *Portland Pleasure Boat*, Aug. 31, 1848.

19. Explains William Wistar Comfort: "The term 'Quaker' was not what the Friends first called themselves. They referred to themselves in the earliest times as Children of the Light and Friends in the Truth. But under the effect of strong religious emotion in their spontaneous preaching, they often trembled and shook, ...So when founder George Fox bid a magistrate before whom he was brought to "quake' with fear of the Lord, he was promptly labeled a Quaker and the name stuck. Received at first with

century, the Quaker faith was on the liberal end of the wide spectrum of Protestant religions to come out of England at this time.[20] Quakers, for example, became known for their strong positions against slavery and in favor of equality of the sexes. Believing that every person could know God individually, Quakers were also against religious hierarchy and paid ministers, whom they called "hireling priests."[21]

Wherever they settled, Quakers erected meeting houses instead of churches. These were of simple design, and looked to the untrained eye more like domestic homes than places of worship. As Quaker historian Silas B. Weeks points out, meeting houses were designed simply to give Quakers a place to gather, and were not considered to be any "more or less holy than other places." Thus, Quakers rejected recognizable church features such as steeples, stained glass, organs, or altars. Their meeting houses were simple, both outside and in, with wooden benches for seating and "Quaker gray" walls without decoration. There was no pulpit, since Quaker services were not led by a preacher. There were special raised benches for the elders, or "weighty friends" whom, as Weeks explains, were women and men "of recognized spiritual maturity." However, anyone could speak during a worship service.[22] The form of Quaker worship practiced was "silent worship," not meaning that they were always silent, but that they were unprogrammed. Quakers sat together in contemplative silence until prompted by the Spirit to speak.[23]

This idea of the meeting house being no more holy than any other place is important and deserves more explanation. It comes from the central Quaker tenet that every person can know God directly and that,

---

resentment, the name has been silently accepted even by the Friends themselves...." William Wistar Comfort, *The Quaker Persuasion Yesterday, Today, Tomorrow* (Philadelphia: Frederick H. Gloeckner, 1956), p. 15.

20. Luella M. Wright, *The Literary Life of Early Friends* (New York: AMS Press, 1966), pp. 12-17.

21. Comfort, *Quaker Persuasion*, 52-54. These pages list in detail everything that Quakers testify for and against.

22. Silas B. Weeks, *New England Quaker Meetinghouses Past and Present* (Richmond, IN: Friends United Press, 2001), pp. ix-x.

23. Comfort, *Quaker Persuasion*, 36-37.

in fact, direct experience is the only way to truly know God. In other words, Quakers believe that one cannot expect to find God in a church, for God dwells within each person. Quakers call this the "light within" and the "divine element in every living man."[24] This direct experience of God was enriched by meeting together, which is the purpose for meeting houses. However, meeting houses are useful, but not essential—early Quaker missionaries held prayer meetings in barns, in hayfields, and by the roadside.[25]

When Jeremiah Hacker's grandparents moved from Salem, Massachusetts to Brunswick, Maine in 1773, they were among the first Quaker families to settle in the region. In the early years, their small group of Friends met in a member's house. Later, they built a one-story meeting house in South Durham, just over the town line from the Hacker homestead. By the time grandson Jeremiah came along in 1801, the small meeting house had been expanded and a second floor added.[26] Within twenty years, the Quakers of Brunswick and Durham had grown to be "a large and very respectable society," comprised mostly of farmers. Their farms were said to be "of excellent order," and supplied the village with apples, grains, and other staples.[27] It was in this pastoral and close-knit religious community that Jeremiah Hacker and his ten brothers and sisters grew up and obtained their education.

---

24. Comfort, *Quaker Persuasion*, 42.

25. Wright, *Literary Life*, 1-2.

26. George Augustus Wheeler, M.D., and Henry Warren Wheeler, *History of Brunswick, Topsham, and Harpswell, Maine* (Boston: Alfred Mudge & Son, Printers, 1878), pp. 42, 867. Page 42 of this source mentions that "several Quakers settled in Brunswick, near the western line," including "the families of Jones and Hacker." Town records on page 867 give the year the Hackers settled in Brunswick: 1773. George Jones Varney, *A Gazetteer of the State of Maine* (Boston: B.B. Russell, 1886), p. 206. This source describes the settling of Quakers in Durham, and the evolution of the meeting house from a private home to the eventual two-story structure.

27. Henry Putnam, *A Description of Brunswick, (Maine) in Letters by a Gentleman from South Carolina, to a Friend in that State* (Brunswick: Joseph Griffin, printer, 1820), p. 22. These are letters from the point of view of Henry Putnam, a visitor from the South, who described the industry and economy of Brunswick in such favorable terms that town officials reprinted his letters in a book. Putnam was impressed with all the hardworking "Yankees" he encountered, including the Quaker farmers.

Early Influences: Farming and the Society of Friends

From the late eighteenth century on, Quaker communities in America tended to be quiet and self-contained. This was a change from just a couple of generations before, when Quakers from England first settled in the American colonies to conduct their "holy experiment" and set up a new and better society for all based on Quaker values of peace, religious tolerance, and simplicity. Quakers had great social and political influence on the colonies in which they settled in large numbers, such as Pennsylvania (named for Quaker William Penn) and New Jersey. However, as Quakers grew in power, wealth, and prominence, the result for many was a loss of their simple way of living. Critics within the religion felt strongly that the more powerful and wealthy Quakers became, the less spiritual their lives were.[28]

Instead of merely complaining about this state of moral decay, Quaker reformers of the eighteenth century worked hard, sometimes traveling door-to-door to convince their fellow Quakers to "give up their pursuit of the vanities of the world" and go back to the simple life that their faith professed. One of the most influential of these reformers was John Woolman of New Jersey who believed that one person's excess wealth meant that others had to struggle. He counseled, therefore, that people should work, not to amass wealth, but to supply their basic needs. Thanks to Woolman and other reformers like him, there was a large movement among Quakers to simplify their lives, withdraw from politics, and turn their attention to nurturing their faith and educating their children.[29] Instead of seeking political power to create a perfect society, as in the earlier "holy experiment," Quakers now worked quietly on "purifying themselves as a peculiar people and reforming their own separate society."[30]

---

28. The previous paragraph is a brief summary of the first section of the chapter "The Quaker Ethic" in David E. Shi's *The Simple Life: Plain Living and High Thinking in American Culture,* (Oxford: Oxford University Press, 1985), pp. 28-39.

29. John Woolman's influence on the Quakers' internal reform movement in the eighteenth century is the subject of the second half of the chapter "The Quaker Ethic." in Shi, *Simple Life,* 39-49.

30. Margaret Hope Bacon, *The Quiet Rebels: The Story of Quakers in America* (Philadelphia: New Society Publishers, 1985), p. 76.

Such was the faith community that raised Jeremiah Hacker. His later writing shows that he possessed an intimate knowledge of the Bible and a solid grounding and belief in Quaker values such as pacifism, equality of the sexes, and rejection of religious hierarchy. Hacker championed these ideals even long after he was disowned by the Quakers.

Little is known about Hacker's parents, Jeremiah and Mercy Hall Hacker, but it is likely that they, like most of their neighbors, were farmers.[31] As an adult, Hacker wrote nostalgic passages about his childhood, describing scenes of pastoral bliss. He remembered himself as "a tottering child by a father's side," catching his first fish, listening to frogs and whip-poor-wills, and playing with "the little group of brothers and sisters, all strangers to care and sorrow."[32] The care and sorrow would come later, when the group of brothers and sisters grew up and went their separate ways.

---

31. There is no direct proof that Hacker's parents were farmers, as the census did not list occupations until 1850. But by the time occupations were listed in the census, Hacker's oldest brother Daniel, who continued to live on the family's land in Brunswick, was listed as a farmer. 1860 Census, Brunswick Maine, (Series M653 Roll 437), p. 942. http://heritagequestonline.com (Accessed Dec. 27, 2004).

32. *Portland Pleasure Boat*, Aug. 31, 1848: 2.

Chapter 2

EARLY PURSUITS: TEACHING AND TRADING

The third youngest child in his family, Hacker was still a teenager when his mother died.[1] Young Hacker went to live with an uncle and aunt, David and Anna Winslow of Westbrook. Later Hacker would remember the Winslows with fondness, particularly Aunt Anna who was a mother-figure and a role model. "Her hand, her heart, and her home were ever open to the cries of want—the poor and needy were never turned empty away," he wrote of Anna years later. "Having made their house my home at various times for more than twenty years, I could say much respecting her acts of kindness and mercy, but the offering of so imperfect a pen would be a feeble tribute...."[2]

It was while living with his aunt and uncle that Hacker began to lose his hearing "before he was nineteen years of age."[3] Because he had only a common school education and was "unfitted...for hard labor" because of his poor hearing,[4] young Hacker chose the profession of teaching penmanship. He moved to Portland where he boarded with relatives,[5] and eventually opened up his own school, advertised in an 1832 newspaper

---

1. Mercy Hacker's death notice was printed in the *Eastern Argus* on June 16, 1818: 3.

2. Jeremiah Hacker, "The Journal of Jeremiah Hacker," *Vineland Historical Magazine*: pp. 309-310.

3. *The Pleasure Boat*, Apr. 1, 1845: 2.

4. Hacker described himself as being "unfitted... for hard labor" due to deafness in *The Pleasure Boat*, Apr. 1, 1845: 2.

5. Hacker lived at his cousin George Hacker's boarding house, according to *The Portland Directory* (Portland, ME: Arthur Shirley, 1834), p. 68.

as "J. Hacker's School" on Maine Street (now Congress Street). Tuition was five dollars for a twelve-week session. Hacker offered classes in daytime as well as evening.[6]

While penmanship instruction may sound like an obscure career choice by modern standards, it was not so uncommon in nineteenth-century Portland. Penmanship was not only a useful skill for business, but also was considered a skill of refinement in the days when calling cards and correspondence by mail were the essential ingredients of social life. Penmanship was taught at small private schools or in tutorials. In fact, there was a plethora of private schools in Portland where one could learn everything from penmanship to pugilism, law to Italian, "moral discipline" to the "correction of stuttering," astronomy to artificial flower making. Penmanship was one of the more popular subjects offered, and Hacker was one of many penmanship instructors advertised in the *Portland Advertiser* and the *Eastern Argus* in the first half of the nineteenth century.[7]

Hacker's cousin, John Neal,[8] was a well-known novelist and editor from Portland and also got his start teaching penmanship. In his autobiography, he recounted how he left a retail job in Portland in his youth and "ran off with a writing-master, who had captivated me; first, by his magnificent penmanship and gentlemanly manners; and next, by

---

6. Details about "J. Hacker's School" are from an ad placed in the *Eastern Argus*, Sept. 18, 1832: 3.

7. William B. Jordan, *Index to Portland Newspapers*, 1785-1835 (Bowie, MD: Heritage Books, 1994), pp. 300-5. This painstakingly-compiled and thorough index includes even the names of individuals who advertised in the newspapers. It shows at least twelve different instructors advertising penmanship classes in Portland between 1810 and 1835, as well as instructors advertising the other subjects listed in the text.

8. John Neal (1795-1876) was Hacker's cousin on his mother's side. Born to Quaker parents, John and Rachel (Hall) Neal of Portland, he lived most of his life in Portland except for some years spent in Boston and London as a young adult. Neal was a lawyer, artist, boxer, women's rights advocate, novelist, essayist, and editor for numerous publications. He is most remembered for his work as an art critic, and for promoting writers and artists. Neal helped make nineteenth-century Portland an art center that rivaled the larger city of Boston. See: William David Barry, *Maine: The Wilder Half of New England* (Gardiner, ME: Tillbury House Publishers, 2012), pp. 103-104.

promising me five hundred dollars a year." Neal was eager to travel and see the country with his new-found mentor; they taught twelve-week classes wherever they went. They only made it as far as Portsmouth, New Hampshire, however, before Neal decided that his employer was "untrustworthy, and a downright adventurer."[9] He left penmanship to pursue other ventures.

Still, John Neal's brief career teaching penmanship provides a glimpse into the profession as it existed in the early 1800s. While in Brunswick, Neal gave lessons to college students as well as to "a number of private inquirers; some of whom had never had a pen in their hands." He taught one woman to write her name so that not only her husband could read it, but so she could read it as well when "written at full length, in large letters." Thus, penmanship instructors were called on to teach basic literacy as well when the situation required.

Hacker did not write in great detail about his own early professional experience, though he taught longer than his cousin John did. He eventually branched out from penmanship and became schoolmaster of a private school for boys. Years later, when he was working as a journalist, Hacker received a letter from a former student who could "remember when [Hacker] drilled instruction into the dull heads of those who loved to play better than study." He fondly remembered the "scenes of that old school room, and of the play yard where we mingled together as boys...."[10] Hacker himself wrote later of his teaching experience that he was "so deaf" that he "could not hear one word in ten of general conversation, yet all went on regular in school and satisfaction was given to parents and scholars."[11]

His hearing, however, continued to deteriorate. Throughout this time, Hacker "spent money on physicians, and on quack medicine"

---

9. John Neal, *Wandering Recollections of a Somewhat Busy Life* (Boston: Roberts Brothers, 1869), p. 129.

10. Letter reprinted in *The Pleasure Boat*, July 14, 1845: 1.

11. Jeremiah Hacker, "The Journal of Jeremiah Hacker," *Vineland Historical Magazine* (Vineland, NJ: Vineland Historical and Antiquarian Society, 1932), p. 207.

advertised in the *Eastern Argus*, with the hope of regaining his hearing.[12] In the end, the medicine did nothing but make him poor. When he became too deaf to teach, he had to seek out other employment. Years later, as a journalist, Hacker would use the power of the press to get his revenge on quack doctors. In the meantime, young Hacker cut his losses by turning his attention to shop-keeping.

In the 1840 *Portland Directory*, Hacker was listed as a trader with a shop on Danforth Street. What he sold in his shop is a bit of a mystery, because his journal doesn't dwell on such details. Hacker certainly had connections to the shipping industry. His younger brother Isaac was a shipmaster, and the brothers had previously boarded together.[13] Portland at the time was a bustling international port—merchants and businessmen traded with such far-off places as Europe, Africa, South America, and the Caribbean islands. Nineteenth-century Portlanders were involved in the "Triangular Trade" that history books tell us about. Salt shipped in from England was brought to Maine ports and used to preserve the cod that were hauled from Maine waters, which were then shipped to New Orleans and other southern ports. Salted cod was a cheap source of protein for the slaves on the cotton plantations of the South. The cod was traded for cotton, which was shipped to England and traded for salt again.[14] Portlanders also engaged in trade with Caribbean ports:

---

12. *The Pleasure Boat*, Apr. 1, 1845: 2

13. According to the *Portland Directory*, (Portland, ME: A. Shirley, 1837), p. 33, Jeremiah Hacker, school-master, and Isaac Hacker, ship-master, boarded with a Nancy Hacker on Cross Street.

14. The following source outlines the triangular trade Mainers engaged in: Stephen J. Hornsby & Wayne M. O'Leary, "Maritime Trade," *Historical Atlas of Maine*, ed. Stephen J. Hornsby and Richard W. Judd (Orono, ME: The University of Maine Press, 2015), plate 34. The long association between the cod fishery and slavery was brought to light by historian Mark Kurlansky. Not only did the cod fishery supply plantations with a cheap food source, but early New England cod traders "facilitated the trade in Africans. In West Africa, slaves could be purchased with cured cod, and to this day there is still a West African market for salt cod and stockfish." Mark Kurlansky, *Cod: A Biography of the Fish that Changed the World*, (New York: Penguin Books, 1997), pp. 82-83.

lumber from Maine was traded for molasses and sugar from the slave plantations of Cuba or Barbados.[15]

From his later writings, we know that Hacker was opposed to supporting slavery in any way, and this extended as well to the products of slavery such as cotton and molasses. He was also opposed to rum, the drink distilled from molasses and sold in grog shops throughout the city. It is therefore unlikely that Hacker was involved in the lucrative triangular or molasses trades; his store was not on the docks like those traders' were.[16] Hacker's Danforth Street shop was on the outskirts of the retail district of the city, in a working class residential district. It is possible he was a wholesaler of bulk goods.[17]

In any case, that particular business venture was short-lived. A turn in the stock market hurt Hacker's business.[18] Added to this was the personal tragedy of the death of his brother Isaac, lost at sea in 1840 at the age of thirty-five.[19] Isaac's death weighed heavily on his thirty-nine-year-old brother. He wrote of it years later:

> That dear brother nearest my own age, who had been my companion, my school mate, my bed-fellow in childhood and youth—the sharer of my sports, my joys and my sorrows, but whose body was buried alive in the broad, deep ocean, where was he? ...I could not bring him home—could think of him only as gone and lost forever.[20]

---

15. Stephen J. Hornsby & Wayne M. O'Leary, "Maritime Trade," *Historical Atlas of Maine*, ed. Stephen J. Hornsby and Richard W. Judd (Orono: The University of Maine Press, 2015), plate 34.

16. Martyn J. Bowden, "Mercantile Portland," *Historical Atlas of Maine*, ed. Stephen J. Hornsby and Richard W. Judd (Orono, ME: The University of Maine Press, 2015), plate 36.

17. Ibid.

18. *The Pleasure Boat*, Apr. 1, 1845: 2.

19. According to cemetery records, Isaac Hacker's headstone in Pine Grove Cemetery stated he was lost at sea in 1840. "Pine Grove Cemetery," *Brunswick Area Cemetery Records* (Brunswick, ME: Pejepscot Historical Society, n.d.), p. 13.

20. *Chariot of Wisdom and Love*, Sept. 19, 1864: 2-3.

Spiritually, it was a low point in Hacker's life. "I was engaged in a store which was a great burden to my mind," he reminisced in his journal:

> O! how fervently did I promise that if the Heavenly Father would liberate me, I would be more faithful. In the spring of 1841 after I had become reduced in my mind to such a degree that my daily supplication was "Save Lord or I perish," a stranger came into my store, and bought all I had in it, thus liberating me for a time from worldly cares.[21]

This was the liberation Hacker had been praying for, and marked a turning point in his life.

---

21. Hacker, "Journal," 207.

Chapter 3

"A Stranger, Among Strangers in Truth": Hacker the Missionary

With the sale of every last item in his shop, Hacker was relieved of his responsibilities—and his livelihood. For many years after this, he lived in near poverty while he worked, not for material needs, but for his soul and the souls of others. By 1843, Hacker had become a full-time missionary, traveling around the state of Maine proselytizing and preaching. He saw this as a calling, not a job. He charged no money because, as he often wrote, the truth was free.[1]

There were two historically significant events in the 1840s that likely affected Hacker's decision to take to the road and spread his particular message. These were the Second Great Awakening and the Wilberite-Gurneyite controversy among the Quakers. The Second Great Awakening was the second widespread series of Protestant religious revivals in America following the Great Awakening of the 1730s and 40s. During the revivals known as the Second Great Awakening, which occurred roughly between the 1790s and the 1840s,[2] itinerant missionaries scoured the countryside preaching to eager crowds and looking for converts. People all over rural America spent many an evening listening

---

1. Hacker, "Journal," 235. Hacker's journal only details his last six months on the road, from July to November 1844. On August 17, he wrote that he "had been traveling a year and a half," which indicates that he started traveling and preaching early in 1843.

2. Elizabeth Elkin Grammer, *Some Wild Visions: Autobiographies by Female Itinerant Evangelists in Nineteenth-Century America* (Oxford: Oxford University Press, 2003), p. 4.

to speakers and looking for something to believe in. Church congregations were repopulating as a result. Presbyterians and Congregationalists were particularly successful at gaining converts during this time,[3] but representatives from nearly all Protestant religions were preaching widely as well, including representatives of some new and controversial millenarian sects such as the Millerites. This outbreak of religious fervor bothered Hacker, who distrusted organized religion no matter what the denomination. Hacker felt that organized religion distracted people from what he called "pure religion," by which he meant the unadulterated, individual relationship a person has with God. During this period, even the Quakers were becoming too organized for Hacker's taste.

There was much controversy among Quakers in the 1840s, as meetings all over New England and elsewhere were becoming divided over the divergent teachings of Joseph John Gurney of England and John Wilbur of Rhode Island. Gurney was the charismatic leader of an evangelical movement in England in which Quakers had begun to formalize their worship services, as in other churches. These changes included reading written prayers, singing hymns, and in some cases even hiring paid ministers. Gurney visited New England in 1838-40 and his ideas spread quickly there.[4] Quakers who adopted Gurney's new ways of worship became known as Gurneyites, or the "Larger Body," because they were soon the majority in New England.[5]

John Wilbur, a Quaker from Rhode Island, became a staunch defender of "primitive Quakerism," which was characterized by holding to Quakers' traditional silent worship. Because of Gurney's great appeal among New England Quakers, Wilbur was disowned by his own meeting, whereupon he broke off and formed a small group of traditional Quakers who were referred to as the Wilburites, or the "Smaller Body." There were only a few thousand Wilburites, and they lived primarily in New

---

3. Mark A. Noll, *America's God: from Jonathan Edwards to Abraham Lincoln* (Oxford, Oxford University Press, 2002), p. 567.

4. Weeks, *Quaker Meetinghouses*, pp. 19-20.

5. Richard D. Stattler, *Guide to the Records of the Religious Society of Friends (Quakers) in New England* (Providence: Rhode Island Historical Society, 1997), p. 15.

England and Ohio.⁶ Thus, New England found itself in the middle of the great divide between the Gurneyites and the Wilburites. One striking example of this divide was exhibited at the monthly meeting in Casco, Maine. It was so divided that the meeting house itself was physically split in two. The right side of the building was a plain room with high-backed benches used for the Wilburites' silent worship. The left side had elaborately carved pews and a reed organ in the front, which reflected the Gurneyites' newer style of worship.⁷

Based on Hacker's views on religion, he would have been more aligned with the Wilburites than the Gurneyites. He believed that silent, unprogrammed worship led by ordinary people and not by ministers was best, but he saw the vast majority of Maine Friends, including those in his family's meeting at Durham, adopt Gurney's new ways of worship.⁸ It is not clear exactly when Hacker was "written out" of his monthly meeting, but he certainly was disowned at some point in the 1840s. It probably occurred either before or during his missionary tour through Maine, which he undertook without the consent of his meeting's Elders.⁹ This disownment left Hacker free to criticize all organized religions, including his own.

There were Quaker missionaries at the time of the Second Great Awakening, as there had been throughout Quaker history. Known as "public ministers," they were recognized by the Elders of their meetings as having a personal message that was particularly beneficial for others to hear.¹⁰ Hacker, who represented only his own views on religion, was not one of them. Some of the towns he visited on his travels had a strong

---

6. Comfort, *Quaker Persuasion*, 36-37; Stattler, *Guide to Records*, 15.

7. Weeks, *Quaker Meetinghouses*, 19-20.

8. Stattler, *Guide to Records*, 37-95. This source lists all of the monthly meetings in New England, and the type of meeting they became during the Gurneyite/Wilburite division (1845-1945). Of the twelve monthly meetings in existence at this time in Maine, only one was identified as a Wilburite meeting. This meeting was in North Berwick, which had split from the Berwick Monthly Meeting and become Gurneyite.

9. This is the reason Hacker gave for why he was disowned. *The Pleasure Boat*, Nov. 3, 1845: 1.

10. Shi, *Simple Life*, 40.

Quaker presence, and he preached to them about leaving their formal religion behind, just as he preached to other denominations.[11] Still, he owed most of his ideas to the religion in which he had been raised, and he gained inspiration from early Quaker missionaries, beginning with founder George Fox. Many of these ministers had been imprisoned, and some were even tortured and hanged for their undeterred spreading of what was described in Quaker literature simply as "the Truth."[12]

What was Hacker's experience on the road, spreading "the Truth," in the midst of the Second Great Awakening? His journal provides a vivid account of this period in his life. Though he traveled alone through central and mid-coast Maine, almost everywhere he went he heard about and saw the results of other itinerant preachers passing through before him. In Frankfort, Hacker spoke before an audience "who had heard so many doctrines and seen so much contention among professed Christians," that some of them had stopped believing in God entirely. He addressed their crisis of faith by telling them of their inner light, "the grace of God in their own minds."[13] On another occasion, Hacker was mistaken for "a notorious character who had been holding meetings" in the area and had recently been exposed in the newspapers. Hacker was able to convince the townspeople of his authenticity, however, by reading a "certificate of character" signed by thirty Portland residents.[14]

Hacker set himself apart from other preachers of the Second Great Awakening by the fact that, while most other preachers tried to get people to join a church, Hacker told them to leave their churches. Following the old Quaker missionary tradition, Hacker's aim in preaching was to convince people that there was no need for religious trappings such as

---

11. Hacker would note when Friends were present at his meetings, as in this passage: "A number of Friends attended this meeting, and I could but fear as I have at some former meetings that some of them, when they attend meetings out of their own society, go rather out of curiosity...than to worship in spirit and in Truth." This passage also makes clear that at that point, Hacker was no longer a member of the Religious Society of Friends. Hacker, "Journal," 311.

12. Wright, *Literary Life*, 2, 20.

13. Hacker, "Journal," 210.

14. Ibid., 270-1.

"hireling priests," ornate church buildings, creeds, or memorized prayers. All of these distracted people from the purity of a personal relationship with God. True Christians, Hacker said, did not need ministers telling them what to believe; they just needed to follow their own inner light. They didn't need church buildings either, Hacker said, since God "dwelleth not...in temples made with men's hands, but in *man*." Hacker wrote in his journal about his desire to convert people to "that pure and undefiled religion which visits the sick, feeds the hungry, clothes the naked, and leads man to live inwardly and outwardly unspotted from the world."[15]

Hacker traveled from town to town in a horse and carriage. He admitted in his journal that he was an odd-looking person. He dressed in very plain clothing "with some patches but clean, and of a drab color."[16] Hacker was making a political statement with his dress since, as we know from his later writings, he boycotted cotton, indigo dyes, and other products produced by slave labor. He meandered through the countryside staying in strangers' homes, taverns, or wherever he could find a room. He advertised his prayer meetings with flyers and by word of mouth. He held meetings in whatever public buildings were available, be they a church, a school, or a town hall. Though he charged no money, he accepted donations from strangers, providing they offered it freely and he felt at "liberty to receive it."[17] He stayed in the homes of acquaintances or strangers, or put up in a tavern if there was no one willing to take him in for free. He depended on the generosity of others for his food.

Hacker found that tavern keepers were often kinder and more generous than the professed Christians and temperance workers. Nonetheless, he preached against alcohol consumption and supported the temperance workers, thus endangering the tavern keeper's profession. Hacker challenged these generous rum-sellers, he wrote, "in a(s) loving a manner as

---

15. Ibid., 308, 312.
16. Ibid., 233.
17. Ibid., 342.

I could." He asked them to listen to "the monitor in their own breasts which tells them by night on their pillows that all is not well." He told them to have faith that, if they listened to their consciences and stopped selling liquor, "they and their families should be provided for in an innocent and honest way, in which they might lay their heads down at night and in death in peace."[18] Drinking was so prevalent in nineteenth-century Maine that some reformers thought that the only way to get Mainers to stop selling and consuming alcohol was to enact legislation. The temperance movement gained support steadily throughout the first half of the nineteenth century and culminated in the passage of the "Maine law" in 1851: this was the first law in the country to ban the sale of alcohol.[19] Hacker, however, would continue to believe that his own use of friendly persuasion was more effective than laws.

Hacker did not receive a warm welcome everywhere he went. In Hampton, the people did not know what to make of him. "I was a stranger, among strangers in truth," Hacker wrote, "for no one spoke to me or took any more notice of me than they would a stray animal, except a few unruly boys, who followed me about the streets, gazing at me…. My appearance is, I am aware, very different from nearly all people in the land."[20] Sometimes his reputation preceded him, and he would arrive in a town only to find that the ministers had warned people not to listen to him. There were towns in which no one was willing to allow him use of a hall. In these places he would hold meetings on the side of the road as the early Quaker missionaries had done in England. On some occasions, even after he was promised a hall, the offer did not materialize. This happened one rainy night in Topsham, when he arrived at a building to find it locked. He suggested to the people gathered there that they hold the meeting outside. "I told them others in times past had suffered the loss of life for the truth, and believing it

---

18. Ibid., 274.

19. William David Barry and Nan Cumming, *Rum, Riot, and Reform: Maine and the History of American Drinking* (Portland, ME: Impressive Printing, 1998), p. 4.

20. Hacker, "Journal," 233.

as precious and desirable now as ever, I felt willing to sit there awhile in the rain...I was in hopes I should find at least one in the village who would be willing to endure a little rain for the truth as well...." Hacker had no takers, but sat outside the building himself, "holding a precious meeting *alone*," long after the curious crowd had left.[21]

Hacker described holding a meeting in Belmont, in which "the power of truth reigned in and over all, except a few who were not willing to renounce their traditions." He wrote that in Unity, he "spoke at some length, without gaining much relief from the heavy burden I felt for this people." In Waldo, Hacker was greeted after a meeting by a man who asked him to visit his dying mother, as one might ask clergy to do. Hacker could not "find liberty to see her...feeling as though she was looking too much for help through man." Hacker told the man that his mother must look to God within herself for strength. Satisfied, the man went home, and Hacker proceeded on his way.[22]

In Litchfield there were many Millerites, and Hacker begged the people to look after them. Millerism was based on the teachings of William Miller, a Baptist preacher from Vermont who began teaching that Jesus's Second Coming would occur by 1843. Later, the date was postponed to 1844, and then indefinitely.[23] The followers of Miller had suspended all normal day-to-day activities so they could prepare themselves for the day of judgment. Hacker described the sadness and eeriness of seeing Millerite farms with vegetables rotting in the fields, while inhabitants sat "in their houses watching, to see the world on fire, and the Savior in the clouds." Worried that they could not survive the approaching winter, but knowing he could not convert them from their beliefs, Hacker called on the other townspeople "to act the part of the good Samaritan to their neighbors" by going into their fields and

---

21. Ibid., 23.

22. Ibid., 311-2.

23. Ronald G. Walters, *American Reformers 1815-1860* (New York: Hill and Wang, 1978), p. 24.

harvesting their vegetables for them. Passing through Litchfield again some days later, Hacker noted that this had been done.[24]

Hacker's journal is full of success stories from his time on the road, and words of gratitude from people who were deeply affected by his preaching. He wrote about old men who "confessed to me in tears that their religion, that they had been for forty years building up, was all torn down in a few minutes by one of my feeble testimonies."[25] One man in Lincolnville declared to Hacker, "I have never heard so much truth in a meeting before, and hope you will be faithful to your calling, for thousands are suffering for want of these truths."[26] Buoyed by these words of encouragement, Hacker soon stopped drifting and dropped anchor (so to speak) in Portland once again, where he found a way to spread "the Truth" through a medium that would literally reach thousands.

---

24. Hacker, "Journal," 23-4.
25. Ibid., 211.
26. Ibid., 34.

Chapter 4

The Pleasure Boat Captain

The Portland that Hacker moved back to in the mid-1840s was a busy metropolis with a population "not far from 16,500," according to the 1846 city directory. The same directory proclaimed proudly that 176 new buildings had undergone construction the previous year and that over 200 would be built in the next.[1] In short, Portland was a thriving, growing city. The maritime trade and retail district of the city were going as strong as ever. Not just goods and fashions, but publications and ideas from far-off places were trafficked through Portland.[2] If there was ever a time and place for Hacker to preach his message to the multitudes, Portland in the mid-1840s was it.

While Hacker would continue to hold independent prayer meetings and speak before audiences for the rest of his life, the new method he used to spread his message was journalism. In Hacker's time, newspapers were not "objective" media, nor were they expected to be. The idea that journalism should be objective—that reporters should present facts to inform the public and let them form their own opinions—would not gain momentum until the early twentieth century.[3] Nineteenth-century

---

1. S. B. Beckett, *The Portland Directory* (Portland: Thurston & Co., 1846), p. 280.

2. As one example, in the city directory, Bearce & Racklyft's shop on Exchange Street advertised imported tea and coffee, as well as "Books, Stationary, Cheap Publications, and Newspapers." S. B. Beckett, *The Portland Directory* (Portland: Thurston & Co., 1847), p. 284.

3. Walter Dean, "The Lost Meaning of 'Objectivity,'" *American Press Institute*, https://www.americanpressinstitute.org/journalism-essentials/bias-objectivity/lost-meaning-objectivity/.

newspapers were simply vehicles to transmit the views of their owners and editors. Journalism, in this sense, was an important mode of activism. Reformers and political partisans alike were well aware of "the power of the press to change public opinion."[4] Historian John Cameron Sim credits the "urge to convince" and change minds with the rise of small newspapers in America in the nineteenth century. If one political party, for example, started a newspaper in a town, then members of the other party would have to come up with the means to start their own paper. Because of this, even small towns often had at least two newspapers.[5]

Portland already had two daily newspapers and seven weekly journals when Hacker began his own weekly publication called *The Pleasure Boat* on April 1, 1845.[6] By his own report, Hacker had to sell his one good coat to obtain the money needed to print his first edition.[7] Eventually the newspaper paid for itself, since Hacker put everything he made from newspaper sales back into printing costs. As for his coat, he borrowed a patched one from a friend (the famous "old drab coat" by which he was known around town). He lived "on bread and water" in a relative's boarding house on Cross Street, where he hand-wrote his newspaper on his knee each week before taking it to his printer on Exchange Street, which was where most of the newspaper offices were located.[8]

---

4. Nancy L. Roberts, "The Peace Advocacy Press," *Outsiders in Nineteenth Century Press History: Multicultural Perspectives*, ed. Frankie Hutton & Barbara Straus Reed, (Bowling Green, OH: Bowling Green State University Popular Press, 1995), p. 209.

5. John L. Sim, *The Grassroots Press: America's Community Newspapers* (Ames, IA: The Iowa University Press, 1969), p. 29.

6. Here is a brief history of the titles used by Jeremiah Hacker for his newspapers. For the first two volumes of publication, he used the title *The Pleasure Boat*. Beginning with volume 3, in 1847, he changed the name to *Portland Pleasure Boat*. After the newspaper floundered in 1862, he started a new publication called *The Chariot of Wisdom and Love* in 1864. Eventually he brought back the boat motif with *Hacker's Pleasure Boat* in 1867.

7. *The Pleasure Boat*, Nov. 24, 1845: 2.

8. Hacker describes his meager diet in *The Pleasure Boat*, July 21, 1845: 1. Hacker's home address, at Nancy Hacker's boarding house on Cross Street, is found in S. B. Beckett's *The Portland Directory* (Portland: Thurston & Co., 1846), p. 164. The address of Hacker's printer on Exchange Street was printed on the first page of each issue of *The Pleasure Boat*. See also Becket, *The Portland Directory*, p. 116.

Newspapers were not profitable businesses, but Hacker's level of poverty was unique—even by the standards for this profession. He was inspired less by journalists who were his contemporaries than by the ancient Friends: the first and second generation of Quakers in England who, like Hacker, started off as missionaries and then turned to publishing tracts in order to reach those people who would not voluntarily attend a prayer meeting. These early Friends did not see writing as a way to earn their living; rather, they saw it as a way to convert the largest number of people possible. Some of these seventeenth-century role-models even had their property seized or spent time in prison on charges of blasphemy.[9] In nineteenth-century Maine, Hacker did not suffer such dire consequences, but he did have to deal with some angry readers. When Hacker received anonymous threatening letters, he printed a request that those responsible "pay the postage on their letters if they can afford to."[10] This was a humble request considering he did not mind receiving threats in the mail, but he preferred not to pay for them.

What made *The Pleasure Boat* so controversial will be explored more in the next half of the book. For now, it is enough to say that Hacker used his newspaper to attack the respected institutions of government and organized religion. He also spoke out against almost everything and almost everyone. He was against slavery, inequality, and alcohol, but he was also critical of the popular reform movements that addressed these issues. He was not above making personal attacks on those he disagreed with. For example, on different occasions, he called well-known temperance advocate Neal Dow "the fanatical Col. Dow," and "a mad dog with a firebrand to his tale."[11] When a reader called Hacker to task for being too combative for a self-proclaimed "man of peace," Hacker defended the "war of words" he engaged in each week. "I believe every man as far as he discovers error or truth, may in some degree, be required to

---

9. Wright, *Literary Life*, 5-6, 33.

10. *The Pleasure Boat*, Sept. 29, 1845: 4.

11. *Portland Pleasure Boat*, Nov. 20, 1847: 1.; and *The Pleasure Boat*, Aug. 11, 1845: 3, respectively.

point out that error, and hold forth the truth. A war of words is then commenced between error and truth."[12] The war he waged was bound to make some enemies.

Of all of Hacker's angry readers, the angriest may have been one "Doctor" William Hutchins Carter. The story of Hacker and Carter deserves telling, because it well illustrates Hacker's character as a journalist. One significant difference between *The Pleasure Boat* and other newspapers of its time is that *The Pleasure Boat* had no advertisements. It was immensely important to Hacker not to sacrifice his independence by depending on financial backers. Since Hacker had no business interests, he had no loyalties. Everyone was fair game for "hacking."

"Doctor" Carter was a traveling physician who, after passing through Portland in 1847, liked it well enough to stay awhile. He bought ads in the local newspapers, circulated handbills, and began selling medicine from his Spring Street office. Carter claimed he could heal a dizzying array of illnesses including dropsy, "female weakness," asthma, and cancer.[13] Unfortunately for Carter, one of his handbills fell into the hands of Jeremiah Hacker. Hacker had given a great deal of his own money in the past to quack doctors promising to cure his deafness and he was wiser from the experience. He wanted to pass on his hard-earned knowledge to his readers so, after receiving Carter's handbill with claims that he deemed too good to be true, he spoke to one of Carter's patients and became convinced that the medicine was both expensive and ineffectual. He subsequently devoted a column to the case in *The Pleasure Boat*, observing that it "appeared to be the production of a humbug or quack." Hacker warned his readers to be cautious consumers when dealing with such over-confident physicians.[14] Having never taken money from Carter to run an advertisement, as most other Portland newspapers had, Hacker was in a position to write exactly what he thought.

---

12. *The Pleasure Boat*, October 27, 1845: 1.

13. These diverse claims are all from one of Dr. Carter's newspaper advertisements entitled "To the Sick and Afflicted," *Portland Advertiser*, December 8, 1847: 4.

14. *The Pleasure Boat*, December 11, 1847: 2.

When Carter himself approached Hacker and threatened to sue him, Hacker continued to write anti-Carter articles with even more vehemence, running some under the heading "Quacks Cabin." Getting nowhere with Hacker, Carter targeted the printer of *The Pleasure Boat* instead. He stormed into the Exchange Street print shop and threatened to sue the printer if he published any more negative articles. Coincidentally, the printer was in the process of typesetting a new issue of *The Pleasure Boat,* that happened to contain another article critical of Dr. Carter. The printer felt compelled to remove it and Hacker had no choice but to comply—almost. In place of the original article, Hacker included a description of the encounter at the print shop. He assured his readers that the original article he had intended to run "will positively appear in the next issue, if any printer in Portland, Boston, or New York dares to print it." He went on to promise, "If I live a while longer, there shall be one free press in Portland, if I have to beg rags to procure it."[15] The next issue did indeed contain the article critical of Dr. Carter that Hacker had promised his readers. It is likely that he went through a different printer, but he did not list the printer's name or address as he had in past issues. Hacker eventually got his own press—in the 1850 census, his official occupation was listed as "printer."[16]

As a result of his stand against Dr. Carter, Hacker gained recognition throughout the city, which increased *The Pleasure Boat*'s popularity, if only for a brief time.[17] John Neal wrote with admiration about how his cousin "demolishes Carter the quack, drives him away, and raps the newspapers over the knuckles as they deserve for befriending the scamp." Neal then went on to sum up Hacker's character as a journalist: "Frank and fearless, wrong-headed, self-righteous, presumptuous and rash, cousin

---

15. The incident between Carter and the printer is detailed in *The Pleasure Boat*, Dec. 25, 1847: 4.

16. *1850 Census, Portland, Maine* (National Archives Microfilm Publications, 1934), Roll no. 252.

17. *Portland Pleasure Boat*, April 22, 1848: 1. By Hacker's own report, the *Boat*'s circulation increased because people who had been "swindled" by Carter wanted to support the newspaper that had exposed him.

Jerry must make enemies at every turn... But what of that? What does Jerry care? You cannot starve such a man—you cannot frighten him."[18]

By this time in his career and life, Hacker was no longer alone. While he started his journalism career as "the Bachelor 'master' of *The Pleasure Boat*,"[19] he had since married and left his room at the Cross Street Boarding House for more domestic surroundings. Unfortunately, we know nothing of the meeting and courtship of Jeremiah Hacker and Submit (Mittie) Tobey. In fact, what we know about Mittie herself is scant. Before marrying Hacker she lived with her widowed mother, Margaret Tobey, and worked as a tailoress.[20] She and Hacker were married in Portland by a Justice of the Peace on August 24, 1846.[21] Afterwards, she must have helped behind the scenes on *The Pleasure Boat* for, in 1847, Hacker began acknowledging her as a crewmember, referring to her as "Mate."[22] The couple continued to live with Mittie's mother in a house on Atlantic Street. This house was in the east end of the city on Mount Joy, presently Munjoy Hill.[23] In those days, Mount Joy was sparsely settled and largely used as a cow pasture,[24] but it was an easy (albeit hilly) commute from Exchange Street and the heart of the city.

---

18. John Neal, "The Pleasure Boat," *Portland Transcript*, June 17, 1848: 71.

19. This is how the *Norway Advertiser* described him, in an article quoted in *The Pleasure Boat*, July 18, 1846: 1.

20. Harlowe Harris, *Portland Directory* (Portland, ME: Arthur Shirley & Son, 1841), p. 94.

21. Judith Holbrook Kelley, ed., *Marriage Returns of Cumberland County, Maine, Prior to 1898* (Rockport, ME: Picton Press, 1998), p. 323.

22. *The Pleasure Boat*, June 26, 1847: 1. By way of introduction to the third volume of the Boat, Hacker writes: "The Owner, Master, and whole Crew of the Boat, except for Mate, is a deaf man that has not heard a sermon for many years..." This appears to be the first time "Mate" gets mentioned. Thus does Mittie make her humble entrance.

23. In the census, Jeremiah Hacker, Submit Hacker, and Margaret Tobey are all listed as members of the same household, with Margaret as the property owner. *1850 Census, Portland, Maine* (National Archives Microfilm Publications, 1934), Roll no. 252.

The 1852 city directory lists their address as Atlantic Street on Mount Joy. S.B. Beckett, *The Portland Directory* (Portland: Thurston & Co., 1852.), pp. 66, 149.

24. Earle G. Shettleworth, Jr. & William David Barry, *Mr. Goodhue Remembers Portland: Scenes from the Mid-19"Century* (Augusta: Maine Historic Preservation Commission, 1981), p. 5.

From this location, Hacker could both continue his newspaper work and begin to cultivate the land.

Some years later, the Hackers moved out of Margaret's house and purchased their own house in Back Cove Village at the north end of Tukey's Bridge, which at that time was part of the town of Westbrook.[25] This house was farther from the city but still a short carriage ride away, and Hacker continued to commute to his newspaper office on Exchange Street. By 1860, the Hackers had another Margret living with them: this was their eleven-year-old adopted daughter, Margrett Hacker.[26] It is not surprising that the Hackers would adopt, since Hacker used his newspaper not only to urge his readers to take in orphaned and underprivileged children, but to actually match children with willing families. Margret herself appeared in brief snippets of the newspaper, like this one that shows Hacker in a much different light than that of hard-boiled journalist:

> There he is now, with a little boy on one knee, and a little girl on the other, and is talking and playing with them. The little girl is aged ten years—has lived with him four years, helps him fold papers—folds full half of them every week, is by his side whenever she is out of school, loves him as she would a father, and never retires at night without throwing her arms around his neck and giving him a kiss.[27]

Margret is one of the mysteries surrounding Hacker's life—it is unclear how long she lived with the Hackers. There is no obvious mention of her after 1860, despite some vague statements Hacker makes about providing for his "family," implying that there were more mouths to feed at home than his own and Mittie's. It is not known if Margret

---

25. S. B. Beckett, *The Portland Directory* (Portland: Thurston & Co., 1863), p. 108.

26. *1860 Census, Westbrook, Maine* (Series M653, Roll 436), p. 35. http://heritagequestonline.com.

27. *Portland Pleasure Boat*, July 13, 1859: 1.

was still living with the Hackers when they moved to New Jersey in 1866. If so, she would have been seventeen.

Chapter 5

RUNNING AGROUND: THE CIVIL WAR, SPIRITUALISM, AND HACKER'S LAST YEARS IN PORTLAND

Hacker eventually forsook Portland and moved to the kinder climes of New Jersey in 1866, thoroughly disgusted and angry with the city in which he'd lived for over thirty years. Perhaps his relationship with Portland began to deteriorate in the early 1860s with the approach of the Civil War. A controversial figure from the time he began to publish his newspaper, Hacker lost favor with many readers by maintaining strong pacifist sentiments in the face of oncoming war—one that many of his fellow reformers in New England viewed as not only as unavoidable, but as morally justifiable.[1]

Historian Nancy L. Roberts described pacifism during the Civil War as "the lonely province" of the Quakers and other "traditional peace sects."[2] Indeed, Hacker was starting to feel lonely as a pacifist in Civil War-era New England. So many people had canceled their subscriptions by January of 1862 that the future of *The Pleasure Boat* was uncertain. "Some were carried away by the war spirit and must have a paper containing the war news," Hacker speculated to the few readers remaining. "Some were afraid to continue in the *Boat* as they thought there would be danger of being...[called] rebels." Hacker warned his readers in July

---

1. Merle Curti writes of the moral struggle of northern abolitionists like William Lloyd Garrison, who had been peace activists but grudgingly supported the North to take up arms if it meant ending slavery. Merle Curti, *Peace or War: the American Struggle, 1636-1936* (Boston: J.S. Cranner & Co., 1959), pp. 113-115.

2. Roberts, "Peace Advocacy Press," 211.

of 1862 that he'd have to stop publication if more people did not subscribe.[3] This was his final plea. The readers spoke with their silence, and *The Pleasure Boat* never set sail again from Portland. Hacker did not sound defeated, however. "We had much rather be all alone in the right than with the whole world in the wrong," he had written before signing off as owner, master, and crew of the *Boat*. "That we are right in denouncing all wars as unnecessary and wicked, we daily have the witness of peace and a clear conscience."[4]

After relinquishing his title as Captain of *The Pleasure Boat*, Hacker retired to his spot of land in Westbrook to fulfill his lifelong dream of being a farmer and considered his "public labors to be at an end."[5] Farming on his plot in Westbrook was not all Hacker had hoped it would be, since his small farm was not prolific. After spending two years trying to eke out a living there, he began to look for new ways to support himself and his family. That's when the spirit spoke to him, signaling both his conversion to Spiritualism as well as his reentry into the field of journalism.[6]

In the late 1840s, a controversial new religious movement began sweeping through America, especially in the liberal northeast. Spiritualism was embraced by many reformers and radicals of the mid-nineteenth century. Most spiritualists were against slavery, against war, and in favor of women's rights. They also believed it was possible for spirits to communicate with the living, which was the crucial foundation upon which the movement was based. It was common for women to play a central role as mediums or conduits of communication between spirits and the living. Spiritualism was a far cry from most organized religions of the day, which were dominated by men.[7]

---

3. *Portland Pleasure Boat*, July 26, 1862: 4.

4. *Portland Pleasure Boat*, Jan. 1, 1862: 4.

5. *Chariot of Wisdom and Love*, June 1, 1864: 1.

6. Ibid., 1.

7. Ann Braude, *Radical Spirits: Spiritualism and Women's Rights in Nineteenth-Century America* (Bloomington: Indiana University Press, 2001), pp. 2-3.

Prominent activists and writers such as William Lloyd Garrison, Sarah and Angelina Grimke, and Harriet Beecher Stowe also dabbled in Spiritualism.[8] Hacker wrote about the topic regularly in the Spiritualists' Cabin of *The Pleasure Boat*. At first he was skeptical, but he was clearly intrigued by Spiritualism and advocated the tenets it preached. In all his years of attending séances and being a serious "seeker," however, he had never seen to his satisfaction any real evidence of communication between the living and the dead. "I had lost parents, a sister, four out of five brothers, and numerous other relatives and friends, whom I had sincerely loved," Hacker wrote, "and when I thought of the intense desire I had always had to know something certain of the state and condition of those friends.... I concluded that if the spirits of those friends did really exist in a conscious state, and could possibly communicate with me either immediately or through mediums, they would have done so long since."[9] Hacker held onto his skepticism even after those closest to him became full converts to Spiritualism. His niece Lizzie was a medium who could interpret the "rappings," or knockings of spirits, and even Mittie communed with spirits in a trance state. Though Hacker related these events matter-of-factly to his readers, he himself was unconvinced that spirits were behind them.[10]

This all changed in 1864, two years after Hacker's first retirement from journalism. As he described it, a spirit spoke to him unexpectedly one day and told him to "Write! Write! Write!" This, Hacker became convinced, was his "spirit mother," or guide. "She told me to ask for no funds, but to go right on from day to day, performing that which would be made plain to me as my proper work." Following the spirit's advice, Hacker knew he was on the right track when he received money from friends and former readers in the mail. He stayed home and continued to write.[11]

---

8. Braude, *Radical Spirits*, 27.

9. *Chariot of Wisdom and Love*, June 1, 1864: 1.

10. *Portland Pleasure Boat*, March 26, 1858; 2.

11. *Chariot of Wisdom and Love*, June 1, 1864: 1-3.

The product of this spiritual guidance was Hacker's second newspaper, *The Chariot of Wisdom and Love*. Running under the banner, "God maketh his angels ministering spirits," the *Chariot* was a true Spiritualist newspaper. In the first issue, Hacker detailed this conversion story. He stated that he was now entertained by spirit choirs and awakened each morning by a spirit bell, though he was too deaf to hear the bells and choirs of this world.[12] In another issue, Hacker wrote about communing with his brother Isaac who died at sea in 1844.

> A few months since while writing a letter to one of my sisters I felt the spirit of this lost Brother present—was influenced by it, my hand felt the influence, and the following was written:
>
> Dear Isaac says:
> "My spirit the ocean could not bind,
> I was home before the vessel,
> And long have tried to find
> Some friend that would believe it,
> And "Jerre" knows 'tis true,
> And now his hand I'm shaking
> While this he writes to you."
>
> And...from that time to this I could never think of him in the ocean as formerly, but often feel his presence and have many times been cheered and encouraged by him in my saddest and loneliest moments.[13]

After moving to downtown Portland once again, Hacker continued to publish his newspaper for two years. Compared to *The Pleasure Boat*, the *Chariot* was considered to be a kinder newspaper. As one local newspaper historian wrote about Hacker: "In this Chariot he doubtless rode more at ease [than in the *Boat*], and in the way of greater usefulness."[14] Even so, the newspaper did not avoid controversial topics. In the midst of the Civil War, Hacker continued to preach pacifism. When one reader wrote in to ask how he proposed that the war should end, Hacker wrote

---

12. Ibid., 1-3.

13. *Chariot of Wisdom and Love*, Sept. 19, 1864: 3.

14. Joseph Griffin, ed., *History of the Press of Maine* (Brunswick, ME: From the Press, 1919), p. 60.

that "the North should say to the South, we are all wrong. We as well as you are guilty." He reminded his readers that the North was not blameless when it came to slavery and that northerners had supported slavery by buying the products of slave labor. In Hacker's mind, there was no enemy to be fought—there was only change to be made on both sides.[15]

Hacker also continued to promote the farming life and announced to his readers that he was looking for land on which to settle in the warmer climate of New York, Pennsylvania, or New Jersey, "in which to spend the little remnant of my days," he explained. Once he settled on New Jersey, he described in detail the crops that could be grown there, which included sweet potato, rye, peaches, Chinese sugarcane, and berries.[16] He passed on the contact information of land sellers in New Jersey as if he wanted to build a community of progressive farmers in the sunny mid-Atlantic region of the country.

Hacker spent a good portion of the newspaper corresponding with young readers in a column that he called Children's Hall. Some of the correspondents had met him in person when he traveled through Maine holding nondenominational prayer meetings, and some had only met him through his newspaper. "I have been wanting to write to you this long time, and Father and Mother say I may, so I will write now and tell you how much I like the Chariot," is how Lizzie Granger introduced herself. "I wish I lived near you, I would run in and help you fold papers, and would bring you some strawberries when they are ripe."[17] Ada May Crosby wrote, "I like you because you love little girls and do not laugh at us because we cannot write good, and don't think it is naughty for us to run out doors and play with the boys. I am seven years old, and cannot write very well.... I try to be a good girl, but sometimes I get naughty and then I am sorry."[18] James Thorn wrote in: "I am a little chap ten years old. My father is a farmer, and I am a farmer's boy.... I

---

15. *Chariot of Wisdom and Love*, Jan. 25, 1865: 3.
16. Ibid., 4.
17. *Chariot of Wisdom and Love*, June 1865: 6.
18. *Chariot of Wisdom and Love*, Sept. 1865: 7.

like [the *Chariot*] because you give the children room in it. I want to write something to let you know there is one boy that reads it. I have read the letters the girls wrote and think they are first rate." He concluded his letter asking more boys to write in, because it was "too bad for us to let the girls beat us writing."[19] Following each letter, Hacker published his own response and a correspondence grew as the same children wrote back and new ones joined the conversation. They learned from each other by sharing experiences and the rules of their favorite games. The Children's Hall tempered the otherwise serious mood of the *Chariot*. It was as if the old journalist was softening.

Then, in 1866, the *Chariot* came suddenly to an explosive end. On the Fourth of July that year, a great fire swept through Portland. It started in a boatyard on Commercial Street and was likely caused by a celebratory firecracker. It was the largest fire that had yet been seen in the entire country.[20] Portland was devastated by the widespread destruction of homes and businesses, and an estimated ten thousand people were left homeless. After having destroyed the waterfront and much of downtown, the fire stopped just three houses short of Hacker's home on Smith Street.[21]

Hacker thought the fire was judgment for the city's sin. Furthermore, he claimed to have warned the city that something similar would inevitably happen. "Year after year, among other evils, [I] faithfully warned the city against the insane and worse than heathenish celebrations usually held on the 4th of July, knowing that whatsoever we sow we must reap, and that such folly and sin would certainly yield an abundant harvest...."[22] In fact, Hacker had made an annual tradition of warning his fellow Portlanders about the dangers of firecrackers and explosives. Never a fan of the 4th of July in the first place, because it celebrated a

---

19. *Chariot of Wisdom and Love*, July 1865: 2.

20. Lydia B. Summers, ed., *Portland* (Portland, ME: Greater Portland Landmarks, 1999), p. 54.

21. *Chariot of Wisdom and Love*, July 1866: 1.

22. Ibid., 1.

victory gained through violence, Hacker complained each year of the loss of limb and property that resulted from reckless celebrations. In 1845 he scolded a group of over-exuberant Portlanders for setting off firecrackers that burned a block of wooden buildings on the night of July fourth. In 1849 he told of men and boys that had lost arms and legs from "firing pistols, swivels and guns" to commemorate the holiday.[23] Hacker's July editions were full of such cautionary tales. Yet, as Hacker wrote in July of 1866, "In return for this labor of love, I was treated with ridicule, scorn, and contempt" by the people he tried to warn.[24]

Hacker's last issue of *The Chariot of Wisdom and Love*, written in the wake of the Great Fire, was a one-page angry tirade, in which he told his readers of his decision to hasten his departure from Portland. "My mission here is ended, and after attending to a few personal matters, the paper will go forth from some other place, if issued at all." He continued, "If means are not furnished, I am willing to step aside, and let louder voices speak; for sin will continue to be reproved, if it must be by fire."[25] Such harsh words put him in the same league with his Old Testament namesake.

His first newspaper ended with war; his second newspaper with fire. Hacker was ready to leave it all behind and start over again in New Jersey.

---

23. *The Pleasure Boat*, July 7, 1845: 4; *Portland Pleasure Boat*, July 26, 1849: 4.

24. *Chariot of Wisdom and Love*, July 1866: 1.

25. Ibid., 1.

Chapter 6

The Last Song of Jeremiah Hacker

In 1866 Hacker moved south to Berlin, New Jersey, where he cleared a plot of land for farming, built the home he called his "ten foot palace," read, and wrote letters to his wife. Mittie, who had stayed behind in Portland to care for her ailing mother joined him in Berlin later.[1] Once the homestead was underway, Hacker turned his attention to reviving his old newspaper, which he now called *Hacker's Pleasure Boat*. The first issue came out exactly one year after the *Chariot's* fiery demise. On the first page, he introduced himself to new readers and caught up with old acquaintances:

> While toiling alone in a land of strangers, we have constantly heard the spirit voices of scattered friends calling for mental and spiritual food, as in the days that are gone; and in response to those calls, we are now seated on the ground amid the stumps with one knee for a writing desk, are preparing this greeting to all our friends and the rest of mankind...[2]

In the landlocked town of Berlin, the *Boat* never quite set sail. Hacker began publishing monthly, but in 1868 he announced that he was switching to quarterly publication due to a dearth of subscriptions.[3] Eventually, he stopped entirely. Finally retired from journalism, except for the occasional tract or published sermon, he devoted his time to farming. In

---

1. *Hacker's Pleasure Boat*, Aug. 1867: 3.
2. *Hacker's Pleasure Boat*, July 1867: 1.
3. *Hacker's Pleasure Boat*, Mar. 1868: 4.

some ways, perhaps, Hacker had found the perfect life in New Jersey. He had finally left the city behind, after years of longing, and he was in a warmer climate for farming. He continued to travel and make public appearances, as evidenced by the fact that he showed up in the minutes of the Pennsylvania State Society of Spiritualists' 1873 annual meeting. At that meeting, he was introduced as "one of the radicals of the age, formerly editor of *The Pleasure Boat*."[4] In the 1880 census, while Jeremiah and Mittie Hacker were still living Berlin, New Jersey, Hacker's occupation was finally listed as farmer.[5]

All the while, Hacker continued to write in to progressive newspapers and proved himself to be as fierce a defender of freedom of the press as ever. In 1887, Hacker wrote in to *Lucifer the Lightbearer*, an embattled freethought newspaper from the Midwest whose editor was facing legal problems:

> [T]his monstrous persecution is not carried on in the interest of morality. Its main object is to crush your paper, and though I do not agree with you in much that you publish, I would spend my little remnant of life in defense of the freedom of speech and the press....I am now in my 80th year. I have spent my life in a war with priestcraft, and in various reforms, and am as busy now as ever. Last month I wrote what, in manuscript, would be equal to one continuous line three-quarters of a mile long, and more than two-thirds of it in mornings before daylight, and in the cause of freethought and morality.[6]

Something happened around this time that tested Hacker's faith in the hereafter. As he got older, his writings strayed from Spiritualism and tiptoed towards agnosticism. He began writing about inconsistencies

---

4. Henry Teas Child, "Spiritualism in Pennsylvania. Official Report of the Seventh Annual Meeting of the Pennsylvania State Society of Spiritualists, held at Institute Hall, Philadelphia, April 1st, 1873," *ReligioPhilosophical Journal*, May 10, 1873. http://www.iapsop.com/spirithistory/pennsylvania_society_of_spiritualists.html (Accessed February 19, 2018).

5. *1880 United States Federal Census, Berlin, Camden, New Jersey*; Roll: *775*; Page: *615D*; Enumeration District: *066*, (Ancestry.com and The Church of Jesus Christ of Latter-day Saints.) [database on-line].

6. *Lucifer the Light-Bearer*, Mar. 4, 1887: 1.

in the Bible[7] and questioning the immortality of the soul. As Warren Chase wrote in an 1888 history of Spiritualism:

> Jeremiah Hacker, former editor and publisher of the *Portland Pleasure Boat* and *Chariot of Love*, all his life a reformer and good worker in the reforms, is still lingering, now in his ninetieth year, and is now in New Jersey raising sweet potatoes and writing poetry, but is too deaf to hear the angels whisper, and has some doubts about a real future life.[8]

In 1888, Hacker was looking to distribute old copies of The Pleasure Boat that he had saved. He wrote in to *Lucifer* to say that though he had intended to circulate his old newspapers for free toward the end of his life to reach a new generation, he and Mittie had now fallen on hard times. "If Liberals will buy these papers to read and distribute among their friends, all will be well; the wolf will be driven from the door for a while. If not, I must sell them to the paper makers, to be worked up into Bibles and tracts, to aid the priests of all sects in deceiving and misleading the people another thousand years; and here, friends, is the question I ask you to solve, Will you buy these papers to do good with, or must they be destroyed?"[9]

Later that same year, the Hackers moved to the farming community of Vineland, New Jersey, a vibrant new town less than thirty years old. It was built as a kind of utopian experiment by Charles K. Landis of Philadelphia. Settling his brand-new town in the wilds of southern New Jersey, Landis created what he thought was the perfect community—a small downtown area with businesses and factories surrounded by miles of farmland. This rural utopia attracted a great diversity of people

---

7. This is the subject of his "Lecture," a tract published in 1886. Hacker writes that the Bible "…comes to us through fallible man, who is liable to errors and mistakes, and as the book which contains it abounds in errors, numerous mistakes, absolute self-evident absurdities impossibilities and falsehoods, it is not only our privilege but our duty to examine the truth…before we accept it, and that is the object of this lecture." Jeremiah Hacker, *A Lecture* (Berlin, N.J.: n.p. 1886,) p. 1.

8. Warren Chase, *Forty Years on the Spiritualist Rostrum* (Boston: Colby & Rich Publishers, 1888), p. 54

9. *Lucifer, the Light-Bearer*, Sept. 7, 1888: 2.

representing many nationalities and religions. Vineland also became a haven for reformers, particularly women's rights' advocates, including writer Mary E. Tillotson and scientist Mary Treat.[10] It is no surprise the Hackers were attracted to Vineland as well.

One year after moving to Vineland, Mittie Hacker died. Jeremiah had two tombstones erected in Siloam Cemetery: one for his wife and the other for himself. The inscription on his wife's tombstone read, "Where Is God?"[11] Hacker lived on for six more years, aided by a housekeeper named Huldah Heacock. An independent woman with "a mind of her own," Heacock was from rural Ohio and had been an avid reader of *The Pleasure Boat*. After separating from her husband, Joel, and exhausting the options of living with her grown children (where her sharp tongue seemed to get her in trouble), Heacock moved to Vineland to seek out her mentor, Hacker.[12] She cared for the aged journalist in a small cottage just outside of Vineland's downtown, which is where Rufus Hall found them when he went looking for Hacker in 1891.

Rufus Hall was the great-grandson of Hacker's sister, Rachel Hacker Hall. While staying in Haverford County, Pennsylvania, Hall took the train to Vineland to find his great-great granduncle, whom he had never met. He wrote to his parents: "I went into Jersey in search of I knew not what—whether an epitaph or a breathing mummy, lingering relic of four generations back. For, considering that he was my great-grandmother's brother and had been totally deaf for years, I could but expect something extraordinary in the shape of a human being." Hall found, to his surprise, a "man of the period" who, even at 90, was still "vigorous in mind and body, and beautiful." Young Hall described Hacker's "silver locks," his "long and white and soft beard," and his "keen black eyes, in which the fire that has burned for nearly a century is as bright as ever."

---

10. Friends of Historic Vineland, "A Ticket to Vineland—The Adult Version," www.vineland.org/history/friends/ticket (Accessed Jan. 9, 2005).

11. *Portland Transcript*, Sept. 11, 1895: 190.

12. "Recollections of Joel and Huldah Heacock," www.starwarsfan.freeservers.com/RECOLLECTIONS.htm (Accessed February 18, 2018).

Living "comfortable but humbly" in a small cottage with his housekeeper, who was "not of kin but...very attentive to him," Hacker played the perfect host. He kept his "thrice-removed" nephew entertained by talking to him about family, as well as "theological, moral and agricultural topics." Having still a solid memory, Hacker had "conversational powers that [Hall] could only envy." Despite having been deaf for so long, he spoke with clear diction. He kept his mind sharp by reading the Old Testament and writing articles for newspapers back in Maine, the most recent of which had advocated "the utilization of the sandy plains of that state in the production of sweet potato."[13]

One might get the impression from Hall's letter that Hacker had softened in his old age and now wrote only about non-controversial agricultural topics. This was not so, however. The retired journalist still exalted in controversy. This can be seen from his last independently published tract, a poem, fittingly called *The Last Song of Jeremiah Hacker* which he wrote when he was ninety-two. In the poem, Hacker returned to his old favorite topic of religion, but this time he attacked not only paid ministers and organized religion, he satirized the Bible as well. Believing at ninety-two that God could not be as angry as the Old Testament made Him out to be, Hacker tried to set the record straight:

> The God of the bible,
> A myth made with pen
> Is known only here
> In the weak minds of men.
> He has no existence
> In regions above,
> For a true god would be
> A pure fountain of love...[14]

---

13. Rufus Hall, "From a letter written to Rufus Hacker Hall and Anna F. Hoag from their son Rufus," http://www.hatevilhalls.org/Halls.org/LETTERS%20THAT'62OWERE%20WRITTEN.html (accessed September 18, 2004).

14. Jeremiah Hacker, *The Last Song of Jeremiah Hacker* (New Jersey: publisher not identified, 1893), p. 15.

On the one hand, those words signaled a change of heart for a man who thirty years before had written that the Great Fire of Portland was punishment from an angry God. Hacker would seem to have rejected the angry God in favor of the loving God, and yet the words, "a true god *would be*," casts a faint shadow of doubt that was absent in his younger days.

Hacker not only published his poem, he sang it on the streets of Vineland. One newspaper reported, "Mr. Hacker composed poems ridiculing the Bible and, followed by men and boys, walked through the principal streets of the town weirdly singing his poems and preaching to the crowds in the style of the ancient Greek orators. Mr. Hacker was very eloquent, and an announcement in the daily papers that he would appear in the public square always attracted a crowd."[15] Thus, Hacker ended his public life in the same way he began it: as a preacher of sorts. For all his long life he could never resist causing a little controversy, nor could he in death. In Siloam Cemetery, next to his wife's headstone, Hacker had his own ready. His wife's stone asked, "Where is God?" His own answered, "The Angry, Wrathful Bible: God Is a Myth." After a peaceful death on August 30, 1895, and a well-attended funeral in which "no ceremony or rites of any kind were performed," Hacker was laid to rest under his controversial last words.[16]

Newspapers around the country marked Hacker's passing, due in part to the fact that his unconventional funeral and controversial epitaph made for good headlines. The daily newspaper in Trenton, New Jersey proclaimed: "The Strange and Weird Funeral of Atheist Jeremiah Hacker. An Awful Tombstone."[17] *The Wichita Daily Eagle* went with the curious headline: "Ten Dollar Coffin Club. One of the Members of Such an Organization is Buried." The article went on to state that Hacker's "body was conveyed to the graveyard in an ordinary wagon…" that "was not due in any way to an inability to afford a better one. He was a member

---

15. *The Daily True American*, Sept. 2, 1895: 1.
16. Ibid., 1.
17. Ibid., 1.

of the 'ten dollar coffin society' of this city, the rules of which will not allow any member to be buried at an expense exceeding $10."[18] Back in Maine, the *Portland Transcript* of course carried the news of Hacker's funeral.[19] *Free Thought Magazine* in Chicago noted Hacker's passing, calling him one of the "pioneer Freethinkers" and saying his funeral "refute[d] the orthodox assertion that 'infidels' 'repent' at the last moment."[20]

But by far the most personal and poignant death notice was in *The Firebrand*, a weekly anarchist newspaper in Portland, Oregon that, like *The Pleasure Boat* of old, was making waves in the radical community. The notice was sent in by Hacker's friend and housekeeper, Huldah Heacock, and was printed under the droll headline: "Died of Old Age."

> Your friend, who was also the friend of every good reform, Jeremiah Hacker, died August the 30th, at the age of 94 years, 3 months and 14 days. He had no disease, but died of old age and without pain.... Like a weary one falling asleep the end came, unexpectedly. What a pity we cannot all die of old age. We did not like to give up the grand old Hero, the world needs him and many more such brave and true men.[21]

In addition to her own letter, Heacock also sent in a poem Hacker had written for *The Firebrand* just "a few days before his death." In it, the ninety-four-year-old poet, retired farmer, and journalist seemed content to set his sights on the valley around him instead of on the mountaintops—spiritually or otherwise. This was truly Jeremiah Hacker's last song.

---

18. *The Wichita Daily Eagle*, Sept. 4, 1895: 2.

19. *Portland Transcript*, Sept. 11, 1895: 190.

20. H.L. Greene, ed., *The Free Thought Magazine*, Vol. 13 (Chicago: H. L. Greene, publisher, 1895), p. 740.

21. The letter continues: "I rejoice to see that woman, too, is awakening, and willing to do her share of the work of bringing about a better social state, or condition. I would like to send you some of brother Hacker's "Missionary Tracts," if they can be appreciated by the Sons and Daughters of Oregon. They might be useful in the Secular Sabbath School, perhaps. Mrs. H. G. Heacock, Vineland, N.J." *The Firebrand*, Nov. 24, 1895: 3.

Much in Little.

The tops of the mountains
Are covered with snow,
While lambs crop green food
In the valleys below.

Keep Low—is the motto—
Not puffed up with pride,
For man can be happy,
Where lambs can reside.[22]

---
22. Ibid., 3.

PLATES

John Neal, 1795-1876
Author, Publisher, and Cousin of Jeremiah Hacker

(Image from the Collections of Maine Historical Society;
reproduced with permission)

THE PLEASURE BOAT.

TRUTH AGAINST ERROR---VICTORY OR DEATH.

Clearance No. 1. PORTLAND, 4th Mo. 1, 1845. Excursion No. 1

PLEASURE BOAT.

J. Hacker,--Owner, Master and Crew.

MUSIC.

God is love—a boundless ocean,
Where a little boat like me,
Buoyed up from earth and manned completely,
Sails on Love o'er land and sea.

CAPTAIN'S NOTICE.

We have hoisted our flag and launched our little boat upon the waters of love, and are ready to receive passengers on an excursion of 'easure. We mean not that kind of pleasure which nearly all christendom are now sailing after, under the command of animal passions and sensual desires—not that pleasure which the un-wise, anti-christian Government ship were in pursuit of, instead of being in the service of the King of Kings, when they were permitted by the King to destroy themselves as a judgment for their wickedness, and a warning to a guilty, blood-stained nation—but we mean that pure, present, and eternal pleasure in which the immortal spirit of man lives and breathes, on which it feeds, and through which it sails when all things on board are in union, and the name, and proved to the world that things which are evil may, by wisdom, be appropriated to uses that will benefit mankind.

We will, however, inform our friends that we did not choose the name. It was wafted to our spiritual ear in a sweet voice, which swept gently over the harp-strings of immortality, and awoke within us the harmony of heaven; and we can see no unfitness in it.

The Great Captain of our salvation, taught and illustrated his life giving principle by literal figures, calling to his aid the works of both nature and art, and himself sailed upon the water; and if man is permitted, and even commanded, to sail in vessels of wood, and rescue the prisoners who are bound on board slave and other Pirate ships, or perishing on wrecks, and clothe and feed them, and land them safely on their native shore; we see no reason why our minds may not be permitted to sail on Love's waters, on board lighter boats, and liberate the tens of thousands of precious immortal s____ who are bound by Pirates on board the sh____ "Priest Craft," and "Church Craft," and other vessels of sin, which are in the service of Prince Beelzebub, and clothe them with the robe of righteousness, and feed them with the bread and waters of salvation, and restore them to Eden, or bear them safely home to the sunny clime of endless ___

can purchase or her our food and raiment; and we, having been unfitted by infirmity for te-couring a slave to our foe, shall be under the necessity of making two pieces of copper an excursion for each passenger, and should we find enough wishing to sail with us to pay our boat builders, we may make another excursion in two or three weeks, and continue it in once a week for three, six, or twelve months; if not, we shall sail our little boat in a more private way, until we arrive into the port of endless rest.

MAN AS HE WAS.

All hands, about Love's breeze is steady;
Spread out the sail like angel's wing,
And waft we through primeval bower,
And drink of truth from Nature's spring.

Through the glass of revelation we look a-stern on the waters of time and behold this earth, and all things that are therein, as they first appeared, when fresh from the hands of their Creator. Yonder is the garden of Eden O blissful bower! Language cannot portray its beauties! Angels alone can proclaim its praise! Over this delightful spot the morning stars sang together, and the sons of God shout-ed for joy. There stands man, a noble pair, in all the majesty of innocence and purity

First page of the first issue of The Pleasure Boat—*April 1, 1845*

(Photo courtesy of Robert P. Helms)

Drawing of Munjoy Hill

(Image from the Collections of Maine Historical Society; reproduced with permission)

Drawing of the Old Exchange

(Image from the Collections of Maine Historical Society; reproduced with permission)

Photograph of Haying at the State School for Boys' Farm

(Image from the Collections of Maine Historical Society; reproduced with permission)

Jeremiah Hacker Grave
Siloam Cemetery, Vineland, New Jersey
The inscription on the headstone reads:

Jeremiah Hacker.
Born in
Brunswick Me. May 16, 1801
Died
Aug. 30, 1895.

Teacher, Lecturer, and 15
years editor and Publisher
of the "Pleasure Boat."

The angry wrathful Bible —
God is a myth.

(Photograph courtesey of Robert P. Helms)

Part Two:
Writings

Part Two Introduction: Major Themes and Language Use in *The Pleasure Boat*

"Freighted with truth, from isms free,
I sail on love o'er land and sea."[1]

Jeremiah Hacker wrote *The Pleasure Boat* for seventeen years and *The Chariot of Wisdom and Love* for another three. *Hacker's Pleasure Boat*, the short-lived New Jersey paper, added another year to the total. In his twenty-one years' worth of writing, Hacker revealed his unique worldview, making especially clear that he longed for a world without government or organized religion. Though he did not lay out a detailed plan of how to achieve this, the cause of land reform was central to his goal. Hacker believed that if everyone could own enough land to support himself, and no one could own more land than he could use, there would be no distinction between rich and poor. If everyone had his or her material needs met, there would be no crime. If there was no crime, there would be no need of laws. Without laws, there would be no need of government. What Hacker envisioned was an agrarian utopia where people would work to support themselves, look after their neighbors, and answer to no government other than "the government of truth in their own minds." [2]

---

1. *The Pleasure Boat*, June 2, 1845: 3.
2. *The Pleasure Boat*, July 18, 1846: 4.

In a society where land determined wealth, Hacker's vision was radical, but not unreasonable; in fact, similar ideas on land reform had been proposed by other reformers. Hacker's arguments had a certain logic to them and were embraced by other radicals of his era. This half of the book breaks down Hacker's overall worldview into sections, based on the recurring themes Hacker discussed. The themes of poverty, popular reform movements, land reform, government, organized religion, women's rights, and juvenile justice will be discussed separately, and also in connection to one another.

On April 1, 1845, *The Pleasure Boat* began: "We have hoisted our flag and launched our little boat upon the waters of love, and are ready to receive passengers on an excursion of pleasure." Jeremiah Hacker, the "captain" of the vessel, quickly qualified the kind of pleasure he meant. He did not mean drinking, dancing, or any other worldly pleasure; he meant "that pure, present and eternal pleasure in which the immortal spirit of man lives and breathes." Hacker's goal was to voyage over sea and land—pointing out things that were "truly useful and instructive," as well as dangers—like "whirlpools of sin and misery" and "the Pirates, the false Pilots, the Land Sharks, and other enemies to humanity."[3]

The Pleasure Boat abounded in the language of the sea. The newspaper was not numbered in volumes and issues, but was identified by clearances and excursions. It was not organized into articles or columns, but by cabins and decks—such as "Pirates' Cabin" and "Promenade Deck." Hacker himself was not the editor and sole contributor, but the "owner, master, and crew." He did not employ this specialized language merely to be clever; rather, it was metaphorical. The *Boat* was his vehicle of truth and also a vessel with which to pick up passengers or followers to help him in his cause.

Other language eccentricities reveal something about Hacker and his mindset. For example, he rejected Americanized English and opted instead for British spellings and phrases, such as colour and gibbet. This

---

3. *The Pleasure Boat*, Apr. 1, 1845: 1.

was likely a product of his Quaker education, as he grew up reading the journals and essays of George Fox and other notable British Quakers. His choice of language could also have reflected his resistance to American patriotism. Whenever he mentioned money, he did not use American currency. Again, he preferred British nomenclature, as when he claimed to his readers he would rather "die by the gibbet" than "pay one farthing" in taxes to support a warring government.[4]

Hacker used Quaker terminology when referring to days and months. Days were not called by their traditional names, because these had roots in Norse mythology and were, therefore, pagan. Sunday was called "First Day," and were numbered on from there. Months were similarly numbered, beginning with January as "First Month."[5] Hacker made extensive use of biblical terminology, and this, again, was similar to the old Quaker texts he grew up reading. Borrowing from the Old Testament, he called Portland "this city of modern Gath," a condemnation of its sinfulness. He called ministers of the church "Priests of Baal," which was a favorite epithet of the Old Testament prophets who used it against anyone they felt did not worship the true God.[6] He sold his newspapers on the street to "publicans and sinners," terms from the New Testament gospels, which nineteenth-century Portlanders who were well-versed in religion would have been familiar with, though the term "publican" had long since been replaced by the less biblical term of "tax collector."

Hacker often used tender language, as if to wrench the hearts of his readers and appeal to their emotions. Nowhere is this more evident than when he was writing about social problems and proposed reforms.

---

4. *The Pleasure Boat*, Oct. 20, 1845: 2.

5. Richard D. Stattler, *Guide to the Records of the Religious Society of Friends (Quakers) in New England* (Providence: Rhode Island Historical Society, 1997), p. 3.

6. Baal was the Canaanite fertility god and worship of Baal presented a threat to Yahwism. Therefore, Baal was "vigorously attacked by the prophets from the time of Elijah until the Exile." Paul Kevin Meagher, OP, S.J. M. et al., Ed., *Encyclopedic Dictionary of Religion*, Vol. 1 of 3, (Washington, D.C.: Corpus Publications, 1979), p. 337.

Chapter 7

REFORMERS' CABIN: *THE PLEASURE BOAT* AS REFORM JOURNAL

Hacker filled his newspaper with descriptions of the city he lived in and the people who inhabited it. He wrote of destitute elderly couples with health problems who still had to work for meager pay and chop their own firewood. He wrote of widows with no money, food, or firewood. He described the children of these widows (near-orphans themselves, in an era when men were traditionally the breadwinners) lugging pails of swill home through the city to feed their mother's pig, often the family's sole source of income. He wrote about ex-prisoners fresh from serving their time in jail who needed honest work. Each week he wrote about the poor, the desperate, and the dispossessed to let his readers know the plight of their neighbors and to urge them to act. Hacker gave faces and names to the poor and challenged readers to help them in concrete ways. After visiting a poor household on his newspaper rounds, Hacker would mention the people he encountered and the specific needs they had. If, in a few weeks, no one helped the poor family, Hacker chided his readers for their inactivity.

Hacker was not unique in writing about urban problems. In fact, the genre of urban nonfiction, which touched upon many social ills and problems, was extremely popular in the nineteenth century. Writers such as Eugene Sue of Paris and George Foster of New York entertained readers with lurid tales of city life concerning both the upper and lower classes, including the goings-on after dark, in order to shock, educate, or push a social agenda on their readers.[1] Though Hacker did exaggerate for the sake of making a point, as did other urban nonfiction writers, he did so for a different reason. Hacker was unique in that he tried to get his readers immediately involved. He asked children to donate their old clothes and toys to poor children they knew at school and to save their spending money to buy bread for poor widows, rather than candy for themselves. He tried to get adults to give money, labor, and clothes to needy people. True reform, to Hacker, meant people quietly going about the business of improving others' lives. He asked no less from his readers, week after week. "All that is wanted," Hacker wrote, "is a little more honesty among seekers—a little more hungering and thirsting for true holiness, and a little band of true reformers, with their lives in their hands, who fear neither prisons nor death."[2]

Historian Roger G. Walters writes that by the early nineteenth century, "Americans had begun to generate what would be the most fervent and diverse outburst of reform energy in American history." This fervor spread through the northeast, and engaged an eager population in numerous worthy causes. Nineteenth-century reformer Thomas Wentworth Higginson spoke of a "sisterhood of reforms," which consisted of "a variety of social and physiological theories of which one was expected to accept all, if any."[3] It was indeed common for individuals to participate in a number of reform movements at once. Typical antebellum reformers were educated middle-class urban protestants, described by historian Charles DeBenedetti as "individualistic yet organized, rationalistic yet sentimental, personally conservative yet socially radical, humanly optimistic yet scripturally literalist."[4] The reform movements they engaged

---

1. Stuart M. Blumin, "Introduction: George G. Foster and the Emerging Metropolis," in *New York by Gas-Light and Other Urban Sketches*, by George G. Foster, (Berkeley: University of California Press, 1990), pp. 19-27.

2. *The Pleasure Boat*, Oct. 27, 1845:3.

3. Ronald G. Walters, *American Reformers 1815-1860* (New York: Hill and Wang, 1978), p. ix.

4. Peter Brock, *Pacifism in the United States, From the Colonial Era to the First World War* (Princeton: Princeton University Press, 1968), pp. 16-17. Brock describes nineteenth-century peace activists in particular, but states that they were "typical romantic reformers..." of the time.

in ranged from abolition to religious revival, health reform to women's rights.

Similar to other urban centers in the northeast, Portland was a city ablaze with reform. Some of the active reform movements in Portland throughout the mid-1800s were temperance, abolition, peace, and women's rights. As "owner, master and crew" of *The Pleasure Boat*, Hacker had something to say about all of these reform movements. Though he was sympathetic to what most reformers were trying to accomplish, he often disagreed with their methods, so he never joined an organization. He had a basic distrust of organizations, especially the popular ones, because he felt popularity diminished their effectiveness. He remained an aloof, independent critic. Without aligning himself with any specific organization, Hacker let his readers know exactly where he stood.

Hacker was particularly outspoken against temperance, a popular reform movement that had taken Portland by storm. By the 1840s, the movement had won over so many converts that thousands rallied to publicly show their support.[5] Walking through the streets of Portland, one could step into any number of temperance shops, businesses that provided men with a place to socialize, eat, and smoke without indulging in alcoholic beverages, as an alternative to taverns. Temperance advocates were a force to be reckoned with, as they knew well how to organize politically. Neal Dow, the best-known temperance advocate in Portland, was a local politician who served two terms as Mayor and ran for U.S. President on the Temperance ticket in 1880.[6] Though unsuccessful in his bid for President, Dow was more successful at home, pushing through legislation to make alcohol illegal—first in Portland, then in the state of

---

5. Hacker wrote about a temperance parade he witnessed in 1844: "The procession contained many thousands, while thousands and thousands walked through the streets as spectators. It was probably the largest gathering of people ever known in Portland." Jeremiah Hacker, "Journal of Jeremiah Hacker," *Vineland Historical Magazine*, p. 208.

6. One can read all about Neal Dow's political pursuits in his autobiography, *The Reminiscences of Neal Dow: Recollections of Eighty Years* (Portland: The Evening Express Publishing Company, 1898), pp. 142-152, 322-327, 522-528.

Maine. Known as the "Maine Law" of 1851, the official ban on alcohol would not be lifted until the end of national Prohibition in 1933.[7]

Hacker believed the temperance movement was too popular for its own good. Witnessing a temperance parade on July 4, 1844, Hacker wrote: "The temperance cause is the cause of mercy, but public show and applause and popular opinion form a sandy foundation." He wrote that such energy would be better spent looking after the "women and children who were made poor by the intemperance of their relations," rather than marching to celebrate the cause.[8] Hacker was especially critical of the uncompromising (or "intemperate") positions taken by temperance advocates when they went from using "moral suasion" to using "the strong arm of the law."[9] Hacker felt that the movement had started to make progress reforming drinkers through "the influence of persuasion, kindness and goodwill," until "the fanatical Col. Dow" and his followers got the law involved. This, Hacker felt, was counterproductive to the cause.

> Men will not permit others to say what they shall or shall not eat or drink. They are willing to be reasoned with in these matters, but are not willing to be forced. What folly, then, for any man or set of men to enact penal laws by which to govern the appetites of others. Such a course ever has and ever will increase the evil it aims to cure.[10]

Hacker predicted that under such a law, it would be only natural for "tiplers to drink two glasses to show their independence, where before, they drank one to gratify the appetite."[11]

---

7. William David Barry and Nan Cumming, *Rum, Riot, and Reform: Maine and the History of American Drinking* (Portland: Impressive Printing, 1998), p. 4.

8. Hacker, "Journal," 208.

9. These are the two terms temperance advocate Neal Dow used to describe the two methods he used. Using "moral suasion" to get drinkers to pledge "complete abstinence" did some good, but in 1837 he became convinced that the only large-scale cure for intemperance was prohibition, or enlisting "the strong arm of the law" to rid Maine of alcohol. Dow, *Reminiscences*, 273.

10. *Portland Pleasure Boat*, Nov. 20, 1847: 1.

11. *The Pleasure Boat*, Oct. 6, 1845: 3.

Hacker also wrote somewhat critically of the abolitionist movement. Though he was sympathetic to the cause of abolition, he believed the focus of the movement was too narrow. Hacker insisted that slavery was everywhere. Like many labor reformers of his period, he applied the term "slavery" not only to describe the condition of black southern slaves, but also the conditions of white factory workers, sailors, and other laborers in the northern states who worked dangerous jobs for little pay. Such people, he claimed, could not afford land on which they might support themselves, so they were forced into the "slavery" of working for rich employers instead of for themselves. Hacker wrote that well-to-do abolitionists (some of whom owned more land than they needed for themselves), should concern themselves as much with ending slavery in the North as in the South. To Hacker, ending slavery in the North meant the distribution of land and the end of poverty.

Jonathan Walker, a Florida ship captain, who was well-known among abolitionists for having had his hand branded as punishment for attempting to smuggle slaves to freedom,[12] took note of Hacker's arguments. Walker wrote in to challenge Hacker's statement that poor northerners were essentially slaves.

> As for the white and black slaves as you distinguish them above, I can see a wide difference in their condition. While the one is robbed of their birthright to the earth, the other is robbed, not only of their birthright to the earth, but of their birthright to their children, husbands and wives, and themselves, too, without the ability of changing or altering their condition.

Hacker, who admired Walker greatly, nonetheless continued to argue his point by insisting that "landless men that are forced to the ocean to work as seamen were separated from their families as slaves were."[13]

---

12. Jonathan Walker was trying to take slaves to freedom in the Bahamas from Pensacola, Florida, when he was caught, taken back to Florida, branded with a hot iron ("SS" for "Slave Stealer"), and imprisoned for his crime. Alvin F. Oickle, *Jonathan Walker the Man with the Branded Hand* (Everett, MA: Lorelli Slater Publisher, 1998), pp. 1-2. That incident, along with Walker's lecture tour through Maine, was mentioned by Hacker in *The Pleasure Boat*, July 25, 1846:3.

13. *The Pleasure Boat*, Mar. 27, 1847: 2-3.

His concern for the white "slaves" of the North, however, did not diminish his strong belief that Southern slavery was wrong. "The only difference between cannibalism and American Slavery is this," he wrote. "The cannibal kills his victim and roasts him before he eats him, whereas the Slaveholder feeds on his victim when alive."[14] Such shocking imagery was often employed by activists looking to jolt people from their complacency and into action. There were opportunities for action in Portland which, like other northern cities, was a stop on the Underground Railroad. Hacker himself participated in the Underground Railroad as did other Portland abolitionists.[15] As one *Pleasure Boat* subscriber wrote in, "a slave room for the fugitive slave... what abolitionist has not as much as that. I happen to know some, even in the city of Portland, who have not only one room, but a free house for the slave."[16]

Hacker must have seemed like a prime candidate for the Portland Antislavery Society, which was formed on the teachings of another radical journalist and abolitionist, William Lloyd Garrison of Boston.[17] Yet when Hacker was approached to join the Antislavery Society, he said he would only do so when all the society's members boycotted all products made by slave labor. If free-labor products were not available, Hacker felt that abolitionists should just do without those items altogether. He was told that while that was an excellent ideal, the other members would not agree to it. As a result, Hacker did not join the organization. Indeed,

---

14. *The Pleasure Boat*, Oct. 20, 1845: 1.

15. That Hacker himself participated in the Underground Railroad is noted in his biographical sketch. Donald Streeter, Preface to "Journal of Jeremiah Hacker," *Vineland Historical Magazine* 17, no. 4 (1932): 204-5.

It is unknown how many Portland abolitionists participated in the Underground Railroad, but according to Neal Dow's memoir, it was a network of antislavery sea captains, safe-house operators, and escorts or guides working together. Dow mentioned that his father "was actively interested in the 'underground railroad,'" providing shelter and food for escaped slaves who arrived in ships "from southern ports" and were "waiting to be escorted farther toward the north star of freedom." Dow, *Reminiscences*, 22.

16. *The Pleasure Boat*, Jan. 31, 1846: 3.

17. Edward O. Schriver, *Go Free: the Antislavery Impulse in Maine, 1833-1855* (Orono, ME: University of Maine Press, 1970), p. 132.

it was hard for almost anyone in Portland to avoid buying products tainted by slavery. Hacker himself once asked his readers if anyone could tell him where he might buy "a little rice that was not watered by the tears of slaves, and taken from them without compensation."[18] He complained that if abolitionists really wanted to end slavery, they should work towards cutting the North's financial ties to the South by establishing shops "where the productions of free labor can be had."[19]

Hacker was not an immediatist, as were Garrison and his colleagues. Immediatists maintained that slavery should be ended immediately, with or without the consent of the slaveholders. Furthermore, there should be no recompense paid to the slaveholders for giving up their slaves.[20] While Hacker agreed that no recompense should be paid, his reasons for this position this were different than most. His aim was to end slavery by reforming the slaveholders. Hacker felt that convincing slaveholders to give up their slaves willingly would be a more peaceful solution than forcing them to give up their slaves. To succeed, abolitionists would have to use both moral and financial persuasion, and change would occur gradually at best. While this may sound like an overly idealistic solution, the tactic had already worked on a smaller scale among Quakers. In the eighteenth century, slavery had not yet been universally condemned by the Religious Society of Friends, and many Southern Quakers owned slaves. John Woolman and other New England Quakers visited Friends throughout the South to preach about the evils of slavery and, ultimately,

---

18. *The Pleasure Boat*, Mar. 27, 1846; 4.

19. *The Pleasure Boat*, Nov. 7, 1846: 3.

20. William Lloyd Garrison was the primary author of the American Anti-Slavery Society's Declaration of Sentiments which read, "Therefore we believe and affirm... that the slaves ought instantly to be set free, and brought under protection of the law." The declaration went on to state that "freeing the slaves is not depriving slaveholders of property, but restoring it to the right owner—it is not wronging the master, but righting the slave—restoring him to himself;
"Because if compensation is to be given at all, it should be given to the outraged and guiltless slaves, and not to those who have plundered and abused them." This outlines the basic principles of the immediatist platform.
"American Anti-Slavery Society Declaration of Sentiments (1833)." *The Radical Reader: a Documentary History of the American Radical Tradition*, Ed. Timothy Patrick McCarthy nd John McMillian, (New York: The New Press, 2003), pp. 125-126.

convinced them to set their slaves free. By 1780, Quakers no longer owned slaves and were unified in their condemnation of slavery. Hacker, along with many nineteenth-century Quakers, thought the same reform should be possible among the general population of Americans.[21]

Another movement Hacker gave only partial support to was women's suffrage. This movement did not officially take off in Maine until the formation of the Maine Woman Suffrage Association in 1873, which actively petitioned the state legislature to allow women to vote. However, the issue was on the minds of many Maine women and like-minded men long before that time, and was the topic of many speeches and much literature. Hacker's cousin, John Neal, spoke out and wrote in favor of suffrage. National suffrage leader Susan B. Anthony had visited Maine in 1857 to generate support for the cause.[22]

Hacker was aware of the small but growing movement and he provided space in his newspaper for readers to express their support for suffrage. Yet, as a nonvoter, Hacker was not an avid supporter of voting rights for anybody. He walked a tightrope—he believed in the equality of women, but he did not believe in the government—therefore, he did not want to encourage anyone to vote. He summed up his position thus:

> As for voting, I do not believe in it for either sex.... Nevertheless, if people will rule by majority, I see no reason why women have not as good a right as men, to vote. Women as well as men are expected to be subject to law...why have they not the same right as men have, to say what those laws shall be...[23]

Hacker was much more decisive in his support of other less political rights for women, and this will be addressed more fully in chapter 11.

---

21. David E. Shi, *The Simple Life: Plain Living and High Thinking in American Culture* (Oxford: Oxford University Press, 1985), pp. 40-41; New England Yearly Meeting, *Faith and Practice of New England Yearly Meeting of Friends* (Worcester, MA: New England Yearly Meeting of Friends, 1986), p. 39.

22. Edward O. Schriver and Stanley R. Howe, "The Republican Ascendancy: Politics and Reform." in *Maine: the Pine Tree State from Prehistory to the Present* (Orono: University of Maine Press, 1995), pp. 386-387.

23. *Portland Pleasure Boat*, Jan.5, 1859: 2.

Chapter 8

FREE LAND OFFICE: HACKER ON LAND REFORM

Romantic reformers of the nineteenth century regarded growing cities to be the cause of many problems. According to Walters, "the cities were especially ripe for moral crusades. Reformers regarded them—with only a bit of exaggeration—as dismal swamps of vice, disease, and misery."[1] Like his contemporaries, Hacker, too, disdained the city. He wrote many pieces that condemned city life, telling his readers that, "In cities the air is impure, water is impure, much of the food is impure, many of the customs and habits of city life are impure." He claimed that cities were places where people learned bad habits and were driven to early graves. "The lives of each generation of those that dwell in cities become shorter until the families die out.... Were it not for the new recruits from the country cities would become extinct."[2]

Hacker confided to his readers that, if he had lived the life he wanted to, he would live "in peace" in the country as a farmer but, as he put it, "more 'hacking' remains to be done...."[3] As a journalist, Hacker could see no alternative to living in the city. "I feel required to be here in the centre of the city, where I can run into taverns, stores, grog shops, and through the streets every leisure moment, selling or giving away papers."[4] Hacker also mentioned another motive for living in the city: he had

---

1. Walters, *American Reformers*, 6.
2. *Portland Pleasure Boat*, Dec. 27, 1849: 1.
3. *Portland Pleasure Boat*, June 19, 1847: 3.
4. *The Pleasure Boat*, July 21, 1845: 1.

come to Portland, "on the same principle that a wrecker boards a sinking ship, to awaken the drowsy multitude, warn them of their danger, and try to persuade them to step on board the life boat of Truth, and sail for the port of peace."[5]

Long before Hacker wrote these words in 1845 about awakening and persuading the drowsy multitude to flee the dangerous city for the peaceful country, the opposite migration was already underway. This was a movement which Hacker, passionate as he was, could not undo. Starting in the early nineteenth century, the countryside throughout New England was being transformed into urban pockets. Mills and factories sprang up along rivers and waterways and changed the land in such a way that it diverted water from farmers. As the rural way of life began to give way to new technologies, mill owners actively recruited young people off of the farms to staff the mills.[6] In 1809, Hacker's old hometown of Brunswick, along the Androscoggin River, was the first town in Maine to erect a cotton mill.[7] Soon to follow were mills in Lewiston, Biddeford, Saco, and York.[8] In 1846, Hacker visited a textile mill in Saco, to which he devoted a column in his paper. He wrote that while his tour guide through the mill "attempted to show me the machinery and its curious operations…I felt but little interest in the contrivances of man." He was much more interested in the "living machines that are robbed of the earth, and imprisoned there…wearing out their lives in unwholesome rooms, to support capitalists and their idle families in luxury and ease."[9] The "living machines," of course, were the factory workers themselves.

---

5. *The Pleasure Boat*, Sept. 22, 1845: 4.

6. Mary Beth Norton et al., *A People and a Nation*, Vol. 1 of 2, (Boston: Houghton Mifflin, 1994), pp. 279-280.

7. Jim Brunelle, *Maine Almanac* (Portland, ME: Guy Gannett Publishing Co., 1978), p. 16.

8. Joel W. Eastman and Paul E. Rivard, "Transportation and Manufacturing," *Maine; The Pine Tree State from Prehistory to the Present* (Orono: University of Maine Press, 1995), pp. 333-336.

9. *The Pleasure Boat*, July 4, 1846: 3.

This idea of being "robbed of the earth" was a recurring theme in Hacker's writing. He wrote that the working classes who populated cities and mill towns were essentially slaves who worked for low wages and were unable to afford "enough of God's earth to raise a potato on."[10] They were robbed of their "birthright" by the government, land speculators, developers and wealthy land owners, who together made land unaffordable to the working class. One had only to look to Europe, Hacker said, to see the problems caused by such "land robbery." He used Ireland as an example. In the 1840s, the Irish potato famine was at its most devastating. Hacker's readers would have been familiar with the famine—news of it filled American papers, and the government and charity groups sent aid overseas. Those who made it out of Ireland alive were beginning to arrive in Portland and other cities on the East coast. "Poor starving Ireland has been reduced to her present state, wholly by land robbery," Hacker claimed, and warned that America was heading in that direction. "One man is landless and homeless while another possesses more than he knows what to do with. This makes slaves of both. He that has no land is a slave to those who have too much, while those that have too much are slaves to their own selfish desires."[11] To Hacker, the solution to this economic disparity was clear: "to give every man, without money or price, as much land as he will cultivate with his own labor, and no more; and allow no man to speculate in land, nor hold more than he can cultivate."[12] His rationale was simple: "The earth belongs in common to all men—'tis God's free gift to all his children."[13]

Though Hacker was the first Maine journalist to make this claim, his idea was hardly new. He was most certainly influenced by the ideas of George Henry Evans and Thomas Skidmore, two New York reformers who had begun their careers in the 1820s. Skidmore, as a founding member of the radical Working Men's Party, was the first to call for "the

---

10. *The Pleasure Boat*, Dec. 8, 1845: 4.
11. *Portland Pleasure Boat*, Sept. 7, 1848: 1; Nov. 27, 1847: 1.
12. *Portland Pleasure Boat*, Nov. 27, 1847: 3.
13. *Portland Pleasure Boat*, Jan. 1, 1848: 1.

abolition of private property and the redistribution of wealth." Skidmore only published one essay, titled "The Rights of Man to Property."[14] It was Evans, a journalist, who picked up Skidmore's cause and gave it voice in his newspaper, *The Workingman's Advocate*, which was started in 1829. For years, Evans argued that the U.S. government should give every landless citizen 160 acres of undeveloped land, on which to live and support himself.[15]

Hacker agreed wholeheartedly with Skidmore and Evans, and saw land reform as the most important social reform of his age. "I have long seen that a free and unalienable home for every man must be the foundation of all reform," he stated, for the simple reason all problems were urban problems.[16] Poverty, despair, intemperance, and vice were, if not caused by cities, at least perpetuated in them. If all men and women were free to support themselves peacefully in the country, Hacker believed this would eliminate poverty entirely. He envisioned that: "Every man would have a spot of land to cultivate, and a home of his own. Crimes would not be known, there would be but very few if any poor people, and those would be provided for by their Christian neighbors...."[17] Government, with its laws and prisons, would not be necessary.

Once he began championing the cause of land reform in his paper, Hacker realized that apathy was the most significant barrier to large-scale reform. Hacker attacked this directly in his writing: "I have been laboring several years, in my little homely way, to call the attention of the people...to the curses of land-robbery. A few manifest some interest on the subject, while the landless, homeless, toiling masses slumber on, over the brink of destruction, as soundly as though they were monarchs on downy beds or cushioned thrones, with whole empires to support

---

14. Timothy Patrick McCarthy and John McMillian, "Thomas Skidmore (1790-1832)," *The Radical Reader* (New York: The New Press, 2003), p. 63.

15. Carl J. Guarneri, "George Henry Evans," *American National Biography* (Oxford: Oxford University Press, 1999), p. 603.

16. *The Pleasure Boat*, Feb. 6, 1847: 4.

17. *The Pleasure Boat*, July 18, 1846: 4.

them."[18] Hacker deemed it the job of the press to reverse this apathy and to get people outraged about the subject. He tried to get other local editors involved. When his cousin John Neal took over as editor of *The Portland Transcript*, a literary newspaper with liberal leanings, Hacker was pleased. In his words, Neal was "no fawning, cringing sycophant" like the other local editors. He addressed Neal in *The Pleasure Boat*, sending him this friendly challenge: "John, ahoy! I say, John, why not go for land reform? Why not advocate the right of every human being to a portion of the soil?"[19]

John Neal answered promptly in the *Transcript*, apologizing first to his own readers for Hacker's exuberance. "Let us forgive cousin Jerry if he jumps too far—all reformers must begin by asking too much, and in consideration of his honesty of purpose, bear with him." Yet Neal pledged his support to Hacker's cause. "He insists upon every son and daughter of Adam being provided for out of the public domain, AND SO DO WE. It is indeed high time the land monopoly were done with, at least in our country, alike the refuge of kings and people."[20]

Hacker responded in the next *Pleasure Boat*, "As John Neal thinks it is high time that land monopoly were done with, we hope he will also think it 'high time' for him to engage in the work, for it is vastly more important... than anything and everything his pen has ever before touched upon...."[21] In the end, Hacker failed to convince his cousin to make land reform a top priority. Undaunted, he continued himself to "engage in the work." He wrote regularly about the need for land reform, and he even traveled throughout the state on occasion, like he had in his missionary days. This time, however, his message had to do with land. On town meeting day in the small eastern Maine town of Columbia, he asked a group of men gathered outside the town hall "if

---

18. *Portland Pleasure Boat*, Nov. 27, 1847: 3.
19. *Portland Pleasure Boat*, June 17, 1848: 4.
20. *Portland Transcript*, June 17, 1848: 71.
21. *Portland Pleasure Boat*, June 24, 1848: 3.

they had been voting away their birthright." Once he had their attention, Hacker began to preach his message of land reform.

> There is land enough in the United States to furnish every man with enough for a good farm and millions of acres to spare. You and your children who want farms, have as much moral right to a piece of wild land as you have to sun-light, air, or water; but you come here and vote for men to enact laws to rob you of that right, and make it trespass to plant a hill of potatoes… until you have worn out your bones in slavery to others, to purchase back the birthright that you have voted away.[22]

In all his writing and speaking about land reform, Hacker never brought up the issue of Native Americans' claim to the land. He did, however, write that the early English settlers were in the wrong to take land from the Native People. In his assessment of American history, he argued against the glorification of the frontier wars between the settlers and Native Americans, which he saw as resulting from the settlers' greed for the land. "Our forefathers obtained their land of the natives by piracy and murder, and these crimes have been taught to children and to children's children from generation to generation."[23] Hacker also condemned similar practices occurring in his own lifetime: he wrote that the forced removal of the Cherokees from their land in the 1830s was abhorrent.[24] Still, he did not consider that the "wild land" he wanted the government to give away might already be occupied. Hacker accepted what anthropologists now call the "vanishing American paradigm," which was so prevalent in the nineteenth century: the mindset that Native Americans were "on the brink of… extinction."[25] Hacker said as much in this fiery indictment of his country's history:

---

22. *Portland Pleasure Boat*, Jan. 1, 1848: 1.

23. *The Pleasure Boat*, Mar. 14, 1846: 2.

24. *The Pleasure Boat*, Sept. 1, 1845: 3.

25. The definition of "Vanishing American paradigm" and the phrase itself are taken from a lecture by Prof. Patricia Erikson titled "Deconstructing the Vanishing American Paradigm: Native Americans and the Next Generation of Anthropology," delivered at Smith College on April 18, 1998. http://www.umass.edu/legal/derrico/erikson.html (Accessed March 12, 2018).

According to Ann McMullen, this way of thinking was prevalent among

> Where are the thousands of red brothers that once roamed over the regions that we inhabit or paddled their canoes along our shores? Gone down into the dust! Gunpowder and firewater have consumed them! Acre by acre was their land taken from them by a band of religious pirates! Step by step were they driven from their hunting grounds by the fire arms of bible-reading God-defying Christians! One by one have they sunk into the earth under the powerful arm of psalm-singing murderers![26]

So, while Hacker was clearly sympathetic to Native Americans historically, he did not consider their current claims on their land, probably because he did not consider there to be many left. Native claims on the land were not a consideration for other land reformers either, as the movement gained momentum.

In September of 1848, the Free Soil Party made its debut in Maine, at a convention in Augusta. Adopting as their motto: "Free Soil, Free Speech, Free Labor, and Free Men," this became the party of choice for abolitionists. "Free soil," in fact, had two meanings: the most famous of these being that party members wanted the soil to be free of slavery.[27] The other meaning of "free soil" was, of course, the proposal that the soil should be free for men to settle on and earn their living. This platform was later adopted by the new Republican Party in 1854. Under the first Republican President, Abraham Lincoln, a Homestead Act was finally passed in 1862 that opened the West for farming and settlement.[28]

Hacker did not join any party, or even vote, but he did petition politicians on the issue. It is also safe to guess that Hacker's writing had

---

nineteenth-century reformers. She wrote: "Most reformers were white easterners, whose limited contact with native people allowed them to believe Northeastern Indians were extinct." Ann McMullen, "What's Wrong with This Picture? Context, Conversion, Survival, and the Development of Regional Native Cultures and Pan-Indianism in Southeastern New England," in *Enduring Traditions: The Native Peoples of New England*, ed. Laurie Weinstein, (Westport, CT: Bergin & Garvey, 1994), p. 130.

26. *The Pleasure Boat*, July 25, 1846: 1.

27. Schriver, *Go Free*, 63-4.

28. Wendy McElroy, "The Free-Soil Movement." *Freedom Daily*, May 2001. http://www.troynovant.com/McElroy/Essays/Free-Soil-Movement.html (Accessed March 13, 2018).

some impact on the burgeoning land reform movement in Maine. He continued to keep the issue before his reading public, writing about it extensively for almost twenty years. When the Homestead Act passed, Hacker gave it his full approval. He was glad that every landless citizen could now "have enough of the public domain to make himself a farm." He urged his readers once again to leave the city and live off the land. "Now we wish to see every family have a home and be no longer the landless slaves of capital, driven about by landlords, and robbed by shylocks."[29]

Years later, when he was retired, Hacker would count land reform as one of his greatest accomplishments. He wrote in to a freethought publication:

> Through my paper, and appeals to the governor and legislature, I got a law to give every landless man in Maine, who would settle on it, one hundred and sixty acres of land for fifty cents an acre, and this to be paid in labor—making roads, etc. Then I saw scores of farmers, each with a two-horse wagon covered with cloth, containing…all they had in the world—steering for the wilderness. You have lectured in one of those counties, and no doubt reaped some of the harvest I sowed in getting that land free.[30]

---

29. *The Pleasure Boat,* July 26: 1862: 4.

30. Quoted in Samuel Porter Putnam, *Four Hundred Years of Freethought.* (New York: The Truth Seeker Company, 1894), p. 479.

Chapter 9

PIRATES CABIN: HACKER ON THE GOVERNMENT

Hacker spent a great deal of time criticizing the government. Early in his journalistic career he was critical of the Democrats, since they were the political party in power. One reader wrote in to accuse Hacker of "influencing some to leave the democratic party and join the whigs." Hacker vehemently denied this. "What do I care which party a man belongs to? If people will dabble in filth they will find no lack of it in either party." Hacker went on to insist that, with all his criticism of the government, he was aiming at something beyond mere political change. "The Boat owns no distinction of sect nor party, and recognizes no national bounds but claims the whole universe as its nation; and would rejoice to see every party division, political and religious swept from the earth."[1]

That summed up Hacker"s philosophy. He liked neither institutions nor organizations, whether political or religious, because he saw them as divisive and flawed. In a time when most newspapers backed a political party or other organization, Hacker and his newspaper sailed alone. "I have nothing to do with politicians," he wrote proudly. "When I look upon the two great political parties, I see only a couple of wolves, nearly alike in size and ferocity, fighting over the fat carcass of a foolish sheep that has run headlong into their den. Sometimes one is rather fatter, sometimes the other, and when I witness their quarrels...I rejoice in the distant prospect of that day, when both parties will be destroyed by the

---

1. *The Pleasure Boat*, Sept. 12, 1846: 1.

spread of the gospel of peace; and humanity, and Christianity find a foot hold on the earth."[2]

Obviously, Hacker felt that the government's problems could not be solved by putting another party in power. The problem was the government itself. Hacker believed people would be better off without it. As well as subjecting people to "human laws," which were themselves flawed, the government punished those who did not adhere to the laws. The government was also responsible for prisons and capital punishment, two things Hacker abhorred. The stances he took on these matters were once again in line with Quaker beliefs; Friends had a long-standing interest in prison reform and most opposed capital punishment. Hacker often wrote about the futility of the punitive prison system, believing firmly that "brotherly counsel and assistance are better than prisons."[3]

Hacker was against capital punishment, which, though seldom used, was legal in Maine throughout most of the nineteenth century.[4] Writing about a man in Portland who was sentenced to death for murder, Hacker asked, "Why not hang the whole court, who in cold blood, pass sentence of death on the criminal?"[5] Capital punishment and war were both forms of murder, Hacker wrote, and the government engaged in both. Worst of all, the government upheld the institution of slavery, thereby disregarding the value of human life. The United States government and its court system, Hacker declared, were "about as competent to try people for crimes as the devil is to try witches."[6]

Hacker wrote in 1846 that his newspaper office was located directly opposite the Exchange Building, the seat of local government. "On stepping into the second story of that building the other day," he wrote,

---

2. *The Pleasure Boat,* July 28, 1845: 4.

3. *The Pleasure Boat,* July 21, 1845: 4.

4. Capital punishment was first abolished in Maine in 1876. Prior to that, there were only a few hangings. Of the two men sentenced to death in the 1840s, neither was brought to the gallows. One committed suicide in prison, and the other was eventually pardoned by the governor. Schriver & Howe, "Republican Ascendancy," 384-385.

5. *The Pleasure Boat,* July 21, 1845: 4.

6. *The Pleasure Boat,* Nov. 7, 1846: 4.

"I was surprised at the number of unclean birds that have built and are now 'feathering their nests' there. Let us count them." He went on to list the mayor, the city assessor, the district clerk, the U.S. Marshal and judges, telling his readers that none of "these characters" would be needed if people would only answer to "the government of truth in their own minds.":

> If this were really a Christian nation there would be no need of any of these characters. Every man would have a spot of land to cultivate, and a home of his own, crimes would not be known., there would be very few if any poor people, and those would be provided for by their Christian neighbors, without a tax collected by law… If people would but consider what an enormous tax they are saddled with to support such characters as they would be better off without, I can but think they would take some proper measures to get rid of that tax, and turn their attention to a government less expensive—even the government of truth in their own minds.[7]

Hacker's obvious disregard for the government and its laws made some of his readers uneasy. Anarchism (though Hacker did not use this term) was a relatively new idea in America. To date there had been only one newspaper dedicated to anarchist ideas: this was *The Peaceful Revolutionist*, which was written and printed by Josiah Warren out of Cincinnati, Ohio from 1833 to 1848.[8] Like Hacker, Warren viewed the government as a hindrance that should be done away with—not by force, but by a change in people's actions and attitudes that would gradually make the need for government obsolete.[9]

The ideas Hacker put forth in *The Pleasure Boat* were equally revolutionary, and did not sit well with some readers. One reader wrote in to cancel

---

7. *The Pleasure Boat*, July 18, 1846: 4.

8. Crispin Sartwell, "Introduction," in *The Practical Anarchist: Writings of Josiah Warren*, ed. Crispin Sartwell, (New York: Fordham University Press, 2011), p. 2. Years of publication are from the OCLC Worldcat listing for "Peaceful Revolutionist," (https://www.worldcat.org/title/peaceful-revolutionist/oclc/31932227&referer=brief_results). Accessed March 8, 2018.

9. William Bailie, *Josiah Warren, the First American Anarchist: A Sociological Study* (Boston: Small, Maynard & Company, 1906), pp. 125-126.

her subscription, giving as her reason: "They say you are opposed to all laws, and if we throw law aside, we shall be like France in wickedness." Hacker retorted that "with our present laws we are approaching France in wickedness every hour, and for that reason I would have all come to the law of God in their own minds...." He continued, "As long as men look for support or protection from the miserable law they have now, so long will their minds be kept from this perfect law. For that reason, the sooner it is thrown aside the better."[10]

In addition to speaking out against the government and its enforced laws, he also took more direct action.

> For my own part...it is my intention to endeavor to live according to what I write, and I am willing to declare before all men, that so long as my mind remains as it has long been on the subject of this government that is protected and supported by war, it is my determination to rot in prison, or die by the gibbet...before I will knowingly pay one farthing in any way or manner for the support of this thieving, man-stealing, war-loving, profligate, soul crushing government of the United States, or any of its officers, courts or prisons.[11]

Unlike his contemporary Henry David Thoreau, Hacker never had to "rot in prison" for refusing to pay taxes, despite the fact that he broadly publicized his actions in his newspaper and encouraged his readers to do likewise. For Hacker, nonparticipation in government seemed to be the first step towards getting rid of government entirely, if he could convince enough people to think as he did.

It is unclear how much success Hacker had overall in persuading his fellow citizens to stop financing the government, but he did mention one instance where he was perhaps too persuasive for his own good. In 1847 Hacker wrote that some subscribers had stopped taking the *Boat* because they could not conscientiously pay postage to support a warring government. This was at a time when the U.S. was engaged in

---

10. *The Pleasure Boat*, Jan. 24, 1846: 3.

11. *The Pleasure Boat*, Oct. 20, 1845: 2.

war with neighboring Mexico. Hacker admired their integrity and felt the need to justify his own use of the U.S. Postal Service. "For my own part," he asserted, "I am willing to pay the government or individuals for bringing me papers or letters worth reading. I would pay the greatest murderer for doing this and could conscientiously pay him. I do not consider the money paid for postage, as having anything to do with war, and as soon as I am convinced that it has, I will cease to pay postage."[12]

There was one more exception to Hacker's refusal to participate in government. Though he stalwartly refused to vote, Hacker had no problem telling elected officials what he thought. He petitioned the state and city governments on the matters closest to his heart, such as land reform and juvenile justice.[13] And on the rare occasion that Hacker agreed with the actions of politicians, he was gracious. "That is right, the Fathers have done nobly," he once wrote about the Portland city government, "and after hacking them so often and so severely, all our crew rejoice to have this opportunity to heave in with them."[14] These moments of praise were few and far between, however. Hacker was willing to give credit when he felt credit was due, but he still maintained that the government in all its incarnations (city, state, and national) caused more problems than it solved.

Towards the end of the Civil War, Hacker was even more insistent on doing away with the federal government, the preservation of which had cost the lives of so many. "Let none who profess to be followers of Christ or friends to humanity ever raise a finger to save it," he wrote. "Let it fall if it will and perish under the weight of its own iniquity, and then there will be room for a moral and spiritual government—the government of wisdom and love to be established in its stead."[15] Later, he expanded on the idea of "the government of wisdom and love," as

---

12. *The Pleasure Boat*, June 19, 1847: 1.
13. Streeter, "Bibliographical Sketch," 204-5.
14. *Portland Pleasure Boat*, Mar. 14, 1850: 3.
15. *Chariot of Wisdom and Love*, June 1, 1864: 6.

he called it, and how it differed fundamentally from the government people knew and lived under.

> There are two kingdoms or principles which are directly opposite to each other, in spirit and in practice. One is the kingdom or principle of love, and rules its subjects by convincement and persuasion. It teaches us what is evil and what is good, and saves the erring. The other is the kingdom of force, and labors to overcome evil by evil, and destroys, crushes, and ruins. No man can belong to both these kingdoms at the same time. If he is a nonresistant and a peace man, he cannot willingly move a finger to aid the government of force, he can neither vote for nor hold office under such a government, but must leave it to those who are in and of the world.[16]

Basically, Hacker's purpose in writing was to challenge people's ideas about the familiar institution of government. He presented an alternative "kingdom or principle of love" that "rules" by "persuasion"; it requires people to work hard and act morally according to their best judgment, without fear of poverty or prisons. Of all Hacker's ideas, this was the most revolutionary and perhaps the most idealistic. While Hacker didn't call himself an anarchist, this term was adopted later by those whose beliefs were remarkably similar to his. Emma Goldman, a well-known activist and spokesperson for the anarchist movement, defined anarchism in a 1911 essay as: "The philosophy of a new social order based on liberty unrestricted by man-made law; the theory that all forms of government rest on violence, and are therefore wrong and harmful, as well as unnecessary."[17] This is a near perfect summary of Hacker's philosophy put forth in *The Pleasure Boat* and *The Chariot of Wisdom and Love*.

---

16. *Hacker's Pleasure Boat*, September 1867: 290.

17. Emma Goldman, "Anarchism: What It Really Stands For (1911)," *The Radical Reader*, Ed. Timothy Patrick McCarthy and John McMillian, (New York: The New Press, 2003), p. 290.

Chapter 10

CHURCH-GOER'S CABIN: HACKER ON ORGANIZED RELIGION

In order for people to live successfully without government, Hacker believed they needed to outgrow their dependence on organized religions, so that they might find moral direction from within. Since the early 1840s, Hacker had been preaching that people should leave their churches, and it continued to be a favorite topic in his newspaper.

Those not yet familiar with Hacker's view on religion were given a good dose of it in the first edition of *The Pleasure Boat*, when Hacker ran the following column:

> Information Wanted—Has any man a right to spend any portion of that earthly inheritance, which God has provided for his children…on a house for religious worship, while any of these children are suffering for the necessaries of life? Would it not be more acceptable to God, for man to spend money in purchasing wood for the poor, than to pay it for what are called Church organs?... Would it not be a more acceptable act of Christianity to build a house for a poor family, or to provide a lot of land for their use, than to build a Church tower? Will some of the religious papers in the land, answer these questions?[1]

Hacker's sentiments concerning religion were entirely Quaker. From the days of George Fox, Quakers had testified against the need for expensive buildings of worship, which they called "steeple houses," or paid preachers, whom they called "hireling priests." Rooted in this

---

1. *The Pleasure Boat*, Apr. 1, 1945: 4.

tradition, Hacker believed that ornate church buildings defied the ideal of Christian charity. Needless frills— such as steeples, organs, and other finery—were draining money that could otherwise be spent on the poor. Hacker went so far as to call a church "the temple of robbery and oppression." He called upon practicing Christians who frequented these churches to "Repent and no longer rob the poor to build curses, calling them temples...."[2]

Hacker thought it was unfair that religion should be so expensive, ensuring that only the well-to-do could participate. Many nineteenth-century New England churches raised money by requiring church members to rent pews. Those who paid the most sat near the altar, and those who paid the least sat towards the back.[3] Some churches did open their doors to the poor, whom they relegated to the balcony, or separated them entirely, offering a special "ministry for the poor." In Hacker's eyes, this segregation was inexcusable. He wrote that giving the poor their own ministry "is placing a gulf between rich and poor which no man can pass over. If the rich worshipers feel so much sympathy for the poor, why do they not remove their pew doors, remembering that the rich and poor are all one in Christ."[4]

Hacker maintained that one reason religion cost so much was because of the ministers who needed salaries. He claimed that they were "hireling priests"[5] who lived off the poor. Faithful parishioners had to work to support their ministers as well as themselves. Hacker believed that no one should be paid to preach, because the Truth should be free—ministers

---

2. *The Pleasure Boat*, Oct. 13, 1845: 3.

3. Melanie B. Smith, "Pews for Sale, for Rent." *The Decatur Daily*, Sept. 11, 2004, http://www.decaturdaily.com/decaturdaily/religion/040911/sale.html (Accessed August 3, 2005).

4. *The Pleasure Boat*, May 9, 1846: 4.

5. "Hireling priest" was a blanket statement used by Quakers to refer to paid clergy of all denominations. It did not single out Catholics, Episcopals, or any other denomination that referred to their clergy as priests. In fact, when Irish Catholics began settling in Portland, Hacker was disturbed by the prejudice directed at them. He warned his overwhelmingly Protestant readers not to speak ill of Catholicism, because "To me, one ism appears quite as good as another." Hacker admired Catholics for their charity work in providing homes for orphans. *Portland Pleasure Boat*, Oct. 23, 1847: 2-3.

should get jobs like everyone else. He complained that because of the Sabbath laws, ministers were the only people who could work on Sundays without penalty.[6] In Maine, the penalty for working on Sunday was "a fine not exceeding ten dollars."[7] In some other states, penalties could be even more severe. Hacker shared an article he had read in a Vermont newspaper that described a farmer who was imprisoned for working on Sunday. He wrote, "It is a little singular a farmer cannot be permitted to raise bread on the Sabbath, while the priest is permitted to traffic off his wares on that holy day and obtain his bread without the trouble of raising it."[8] He went on to state publicly his own disregard for the law: "I have sold more than a few *Boats* on the sabbath, and if I had not so much other labor to perform, I would sell them from morning till night."[9]

Ironically, Hacker criticized the Quakers more than anyone else in his religious assessments. He felt that the Quakers of his time had strayed from the spirit and intention of George Fox and depended too much on authority. The Quaker elders, Hacker charged, ruled the others in the same way the "hireling priests" ruled over their flock: using fear and intimidation. Hacker's criticism of Quakers may have had something to do with the fact that, as a disowned Quaker, he was rather embittered. But a closer look at his criticisms reveals the same underlying principle that Hacker believed about all religion.

While Hacker believed that the Society of Friends had been founded to free people from the oppression of organized religion, he felt it had become too organized and, therefore, as oppressive as the other religions. In a column titled "An Epistle of Love to the prisoners on board the wreck of the old ship Quaker," Hacker called upon Friends

---

6. In the mid-nineteenth century, each state had its own law promoting observance of the Sabbath. In New England states, the Sabbath extended from Saturday to Sunday evening. George M. Stephenson, *The Puritan Heritage* (New York: Macmillan, 1952), pp. 181-182.

7. John P. Lord, *The Maine Townsman, or Laws for the Regulation of Towns* (Portland: Sanborn & Carter, 1847), p. 250.

8. *The Pleasure Boat*, Nov. 3, 1845: 4.

9. Ibid.

to save what was true in their faith by destroying the structure of the religious institution. He insisted that all religious institutions had adverse effects on individual spiritual growth. Their only accomplishments had been "to nurse hypocrisy...and to trample down the true seed of spiritual Israel...." Hacker summed up his position by stating, "All religious societies must, and will be destroyed." He added as a qualifier: "I do not intend to say that no good exists in any society—for there are individuals in all, who show forth more or less good works." However, Hacker felt these good individuals would be more productive without the constraints of organized religion.[10]

As he hacked away at all religious institutions, Hacker wrote in favor of what he called "pure and undefiled religion," whose only requirements were, "to visit the fatherless and widow" instead of a temple, and "live unspotted from, rather than spotted with, the 'world.'"[11] Hacker often wrote of the need for a space to hold non-denominational worship meetings "free from politics and priest craft, and every ism," open to anyone regardless of religious or financial status.[12] He continued to hold his own religious meetings whenever he could—in Portland or on his travels throughout the countryside. He advertised one such meeting in the *Boat*: "All honest inquirers after Truth, together with publicans and sinners are invited to attend."[13]

Because of Hacker's stance against organized religion, he is associated with the Freethought movement. An old and long-controversial movement, Freethought was beginning to gain some momentum in the nineteenth century. Historian Susan Jacoby refers to the latter half of the nineteenth and early twentieth centuries as "the golden age of Freethought."[14] Freethinkers, also called secularists, included people

---

10. *The Pleasure Boat*, July 28, 1845: 1.

11. *The Pleasure Boat*, Aug. 11, 1845: 3.

12. *The Pleasure Boat*, Oct. 13, 1845: 4.

13. *The Pleasure Boat*, May 30, 1846; 4.

14. Susan Jacoby, *Freethinkers: A History of American Secularism* (New York: Metropolitan Books, 2004), pp. 149, 151.

across the religious spectrum, from the privately religious to agnostics and atheists. Jacoby writes that what freethinkers all shared was a reliance on reason over faith, and the humanitarian concern of making the world better now.[15] Robert Ingorsoll, a contemporary of Hacker's (though some thirty years younger)[16] was a prominent spokesperson of the freethought movement. He wrote:

> Secularism teaches us to be good here and now. I know nothing better than goodness....Secularism has no "castles in Spain." It has no glorified fog. It depends on realities, upon demonstrations; and its end and aim is to make this world better every day—to do away with poverty and crime, and to cover the world with happy and contented homes.[17]

This echoes Hacker's own admonition to build a house for a poor family rather than a church tower. It is also reminiscent of his advice to people he met, as quoted in *The Voice of Industry*, "Be good and do good."[18] Hacker was an early proponent of freethought, as he was writing *The Pleasure Boat* decades before Ingersoll began his storied career as a lecturer and writer. Nonetheless, Hacker would become familiar with Ingersoll and admire his work. This is evidenced by Hacker's letter to the International Congress of Freethinkers in 1894, nominating Ingersoll for president of their organization.[19]

---

15. Jacoby, *Freethinkers*, pp. 4-5; 11.

16. Jacoby, *Freethinkers*, p. 158.

17. Jacoby, *Freethinkers*, p. 11, quoting from Robert Green Ingersoll's *The Works of Robert Ingersoll* (New York: Dresden Publishing Company, 1900) vol. 8, pp. 393-394.

18. *The Voice of Industry*, Oct. 29, 1847: 2.

19. The notes from the International Congress of Freethinkers: "Monday morning opened with a membership of one hundred and fifty for the congress—a larger membership than any congress ever before held. The credentials of the foreign delegates were read, and a letter from Jeremiah Hacker, urging the nomination of Ingersoll for the presidency—Jeremiah Hacker, who, for over fifty years, has waved our colors to the breeze." Samuel Porter Putnam, *Four Hundred Years of Freethought* (New York: The Truth Seeker Company, 1894), p. 660.

Chapter 11

SPIRITUALISTS' CABIN: HACKER ON WOMEN'S RIGHTS

Eventually, Hacker embraced Spiritualism, which by 1864 (the year of his conversion) was practiced around the country by like-minded individuals who distrusted organized religion but placed value on individual spiritual experience: namely, communing with spirits. Ann Braude writes that it is difficult for historians to measure the scope of Spiritualism, precisely because Spiritualists refused to organize.[1] Over-arching rules and religious hierarchy were both rejected. As Hacker wrote, "The Spiritualists have no Church organization, no adopted creed, nor articles of faith."[2] Some of the earliest adherents of Spiritualism were disaffected Quakers from Rochester, New York, who witnessed "rappings" (knocking sounds—as interpreted by a medium) and accepted their spiritual origins, believing that individuals communicating with spirits was "an expression of the doctrine of the inner light."[3]

Though it is hard to measure the full scope of the movement, Spiritualism crossed race, class, and gender boundaries, and had some very famous proponents. For example, Supreme Court Judge John Edmonds and First Lady Mary Todd Lincoln were both Spiritualists. Mrs. Lincoln was known to invite mediums to hold seances in the White House for

---

1. Ann Braude, *Radical Spirits: Spiritualism and Women's Rights in Nineteenth-Century America* (Bloomington: Indiana University Press, 2001), p. 25.

2. *Hacker's Pleasure Boat*, Aug. 1867: 2.

3. Braude, *Radical Spirits*, 14.

cabinet members and senators.[4] In addition to the rich and politically powerful, and middle-class people "of English Protestant descent," Spiritualism also appealed to Catholics and Jews in some parts of the country. The movement was popular among urban laborers, rural poor, and African Americans, including those enslaved in the South.[5]

Though Spiritualism had no adopted creed, as Hacker pointed out, it did have a loose platform of beliefs and causes. Because the movement was based on the experience of communing with the dead, Spiritualists believed that not only the soul but the identity of a person remained after death.[6] In addition, Spiritualists preached radical individuality and believed in "the authority of each individual soul" here and now, and held a distrust of institutions that try to assert authority over it.[7] Because of the focus on personal religious experience, they believed that home, not church, was the holiest place.[8] Stemming naturally from the belief in individual freedoms, Spiritualists were overwhelmingly opposed to slavery, and in favor of women's rights.[9]

One unique aspect of Spiritualism was that most mediums were female. Mediums were among the first women to speak in public, even in reform circles.[10] Because of this, and the emphasis placed on individualism, it naturally followed that Spiritualists "vigorously applied the principle of individualism to the role of women." Spiritualists were among the most outspoken proponents of women's rights in the nineteenth century. While it did not follow that all women's rights advocates were Spiritualists, all Spiritualists advocated for the rights of women. In fact, this was deemed by many Spiritualists to be their most important cause.[11]

---

4. Braude, *Radical Spirits*, 27.
5. Braude, *Radical Spirits*, 28-9.
6. Braude, *Radical Spirits*, 201-2.
7. Braude, *Radical Spirits*, 70.
8. Braude, *Radical Spirits*, 24.
9. Braude, *Radical Spirits*, 73.
10. Braude, *Radical Spirits*, 90-1.
11. Braude, *Radical Spirits*, 56, 3.

Even before he became a Spiritualist himself, Hacker's ideas showed signs of influence from the Spiritualists' unique platform. Over time, he became increasingly outspoken about the equality of women. He came out against the institution of marriage as it was practiced and advocated for a freer union with more access to divorce if the couple should fall out of love.[12] Like some of the more radical Spiritualists, Hacker believed that the morality of sex had less to do with whether a couple were married and more to do with whether a couple were in love.[13] Sex within a loveless marriage was adultery, Hacker maintained. Not only did nineteenth-century marriage laws make it difficult for a woman to obtain a divorce, they also commanded that she always be sexually accessible to her husband.[14] These strict laws forced women into the "adultery" that Hacker referred to, as well as the resulting unwanted pregnancies. Hacker asserted that if the government must "continue to interfere with marriage by statute laws, let it marry people so long as they are mutually happy in that relation; but when they can no longer live in harmony let them separate, not bind them in a system of adultery to fill pauper houses and prisons with the offspring of lust."[15]

Related to their concern that marriage laws were unfair to women, some Spiritualists argued that women should be allowed to work and receive pay equal to men. This would allow women to have the choice of whether to marry or not; they would not have to get married just for economic security. Some female Spiritualists, such as Lizzie Doten, proposed enacting legislation that would require employers to pay women equally to men.[16] Hacker also spoke out against the lack of decent paying employment opportunities for women.

> [Women] have been shut out of almost every lucrative, self-sustaining employment, and when permitted to enter into any employment their

---

12. *Chariot of Wisdom and Love*, June 25, 1865: 3.
13. Braude, *Radical Spirits*, 128.
14. Braude, *Radical Spirits*, 128.
15. *Chariot of Wisdom and Love*, June 25, 1865: 3.
16. Braude, *Radical Spirits*, 120.

wages are cut down, so that they must work from two to five days to earn or gain as much as a man receives in one day.[17]

He saw farming as one area that had been opened up to women and encouraged his female readers to become farmers. He offered to use his newspaper as a resource to pass on information for women to find land on which to support themselves.

> I am now inquiring for a suitable place, where females who desire to rely on their own efforts for support, may come together and procure, each a few acres of land, near good markets for garden purposes, and if there are any who are willing to be guided by the foregoing advice or similar principles, who would like to secure such a home and employment, I would like to have their names.[18]

Hacker was also very interested in dress reform, a cause adopted by a small faction of female Spiritualists. Dress reformers refused to wear the accepted women's fashions of the time, which included tight-fitting corsets, because they were not only uncomfortable, but unhealthy. Women's fashions were considered "morally debasing" by most Spiritualists, because they disfigured women in order to make them more attractive to men. As historian Ann Braude summed up the position of dress reformers: "Confining clothes 'kept women in their place'.... Replacing traditional attire with reform dress indicated independence of spirit as well as a desire for physical freedom."[19] This idea found much sympathy among Spiritualists, but only a few women dared act on it. Those who did traded in their fine dresses and stiff corsets for a costume of loose trousers under a short skirt, which became known as "American dress," or simply "reform dress."[20]

One early proponent of dress reform (who not only advocated for it but wore the costume) was journalist Amelia Jenks Bloomer from

---

17. *Hacker's Pleasure Boat*, Aug. 1867: 2.
18. *Chariot of Wisdom and Love*, Oct. 25, 1864: 8.
19. Braude, *Radical Spirits*, 152.
20. Braude, *Radical Spirits*, 80.

upstate New York. She was the first female editor of a newspaper, *The Lily*, which was a reform journal that she produced from 1849 to 1853. Despite her impressive resume, the thing she became most famous for was "the bloomer," the loose-fitting trousers she wore, which became synonymous with her name.[21] Dress reformers like Bloomer were often subjected to ridicule and most female Spiritualists continued to argue for the equality of women while wearing the accepted fashions of the day.

This fact rankled Hacker, who was an avid proponent of dress reform. As a man, he could not don the reform dress, but he did all he could to support others in doing so. He announced in his newspaper that he would buy the reform dress for any woman who would wear it. Having no serious takers, he lamented the fashion consciousness of Portland women. "I know only one female in Portland or its vicinity, who wears the reform dress," he wrote in 1858, "and she only about her housework. In fact, there is not a city on the face of the earth, where the females are greater slaves to fashion, than here."[22] This means that even Mittie Hacker did not wear the reform dress—unless she was the one her husband referred to, who wore it only for her housework. In the end, though his heart may have been in the right place, Hacker was just another man telling women what to wear—and the women of Portland weren't listening.

One of the things that impressed Hacker about the farming communities of southern New Jersey (where he eventually moved) was that many women there did wear reform dress. Furthermore, Hacker said he "did not see any person silly enough to laugh at them as they would here" in the fashionable cities of the north.[23]

---

21. "Amelia Bloomer," *Encyclopaedia Britannica*, (Enclyclopaedia Britannica, Inc., 2017) https://www.britannica.com/biography/Amelia-Bloomerhttps://www.britannica.com/biography/Amelia-Bloomer (Accessed Feb. 9, 2018).

22. *Portland Pleasure Boat*, Feb. 12, 1858: 1.

23. *Chariot of Wisdom and Love*, Jan. 25, 1865: 4.

Chapter 12

HUMANITY'S COURTROOM: HACKER ON JUVENILE JUSTICE

Hacker did not believe prisons were the answer to crime. He wrote in the *Pleasure Boat* that "brotherly counsel and assistance are better than prisons."[1] He envisioned a time when prisons, along with the governments that ran them, would not be necessary. Yet as long as prisons existed, Hacker would work toward their reform.

Hacker was influenced by a long tradition of prison reform in both England and America. Like most prison reformers, Hacker's activism began with a visit. Some prison reformers' visits were unintentional, as was the case with numerous early Quakers serving prison sentences for breaking Puritan laws.[2] George Fox, for example, was imprisoned on many occasions for interrupting sermons, and committing "blasphemy." When imprisoned in Derby jail in 1651, Fox wrote about conditions there in his journal, describing young girls being hanged for theft and that the prisoners "learned badness one of another in talking of their bad deeds."[3] Since the days of Fox, prison reform was an important issue for Quakers and a central testimony to their faith.

The turn of the century brought a new generation of prison reformers. Quaker Elizabeth Frye from England was one of the most prominent. She got her start in prison reform when American Quaker Stephen

---

1. *The Pleasure Boat*, July 21, 1845: 4.

2. William Wistar Comfort, *The Quaker Persuasion Yesterday, Today, Tomorrow* (Philadelphia: Frederick H. Gloekner, 1956), pp. 16, 54.

3. Robert Alan Cooper, "The English Quakers and Prison Reform, 1809-23." *Quaker History* 68, no. 1 (1979): 3.

Grellet visited London prisons in 1813, and appealed to Frye to help improve conditions of women inmates. Frye accepted the challenging, forming the Association for the Improvement of Women Prisoners at Newgate. She started a school for female prisoners and their children to learn the Bible. Members of the public started visiting prison to watch Fry read the Bible to prisoners, which inspired others to follow her lead. Visiting prisons became "a fashionable pastime for respectable women" in England and America.[4]

When American teacher Dorothea Dix paid her first prison visit in 1841, she was continuing this tradition. What was new was her level of activism. She was surprised to see people with mental illness in East Cambridge jail, serving time alongside offenders. She went on to visit other prisons and found that this practice was widespread: people were imprisoned for no other "crime" than mental illness. Furthermore, these inmates were often malnourished and abused. She petitioned the Massachusetts state legislature in 1843 to remove those with mental illness from the prisons and get them the help they need.[5] Dix was instrumental in starting mental hospitals throughout the country. She continued to work toward general prison reform, but her primary concern was caring for those with mental illness.[6]

Hacker likewise concerned himself with a group within the prison population he felt did not belong there. Continuing the tradition of other prison reformers, Hacker made regular trips to the Portland jail, visiting with prisoners and giving them copies of his newspaper in the hope of comforting and reforming them. In the Quaker prison reform tradition, he believed in reform over punishment.[7] Jails were punitive,

---

4. Robert Alan Cooper,. "The English Quakers and Prison Reform 1809-23," *Quaker History* 68, no. 1 (1979): 8-9.

5. Howard Zinn, *A People's History of the United States* (New York: Perennial Classics, 2001), p. 121.

6. "Dorothea Dix Begins Her Crusade," MassMoments, Mass Humanities, https://www.massmoments.org/moment-details/dorothea-dix-begins-her-crusade.html.

7. William Wistar Comfort, *The Quaker Persuasion Yesterday, Today, Tomorrow* (Philadelphia: Frederick H. Gloekner, 1956), 16, 54. Comfort writes that Quakers undertook prison reform with "a treasure of experience and sympathy to draw upon," since

and therefore were not a good place for anyone, Hacker believed; they were especially bad places for children. He was outraged when he saw children in jail, which was quite frequently, as there was no alternative in place for them in the 1840s. Appealing to his readers' humanity, Hacker often described the individual children he encountered in prison, such as this boy he saw in 1845:

> Within one of the cells, secured by ponderous oak and iron doors, with huge locks, bars and bolts, is a boy less than ten years of age, who has been permitted to run among the churches and ministers of this city, in poverty, rags, and vice. He has recently been arrested for stealing, and is to be tried at this Court. The poor little fellow was so naked, amidst his rags and tatters, the court, or some of its officers... have had him dressed up...."[8]

Hacker concluded this description with this indictment of his country and city: "Wo to the nation, whose laws will throw such a child into prison, and try him in court, to disgrace, harden, and ruin him, when, by a little kindness, he might be reclaimed. And wo to the city that permits children to grow up in such a manner." Thus Hacker believed that juvenile offenders were failed not only by a justice system which treated them like adults, but by a city that did not care about them.

Since Hacker saw the problem as two-fold, he proposed two solutions. First, he proposed to eliminate what he saw as the causes of juvenile crime. It seemed to him that the children committing crimes were homeless street urchins, or at least very poor children, stealing for survival. Making sure all orphans had a good home, and that all families could provide for their children, would go a long way toward stopping juvenile crime. He told his readers in an early issue of *The Pleasure Boat* what they could do about the problem: "Feed the hungry, clothe the naked, provide labor for the poor, with just wages—provide *suitable*

---

early Friends frequently broke Puritan laws "which landed them in jail for indefinite periods." Thus Quakers worked to improve prison conditions as well as reform those who committed crimes.

8. *The Pleasure Boat*, June 23, 1845: 3.

homes for orphans, and other idle ragged children—and, in short, learn to do as well as *say*."⁹

To this end, Hacker did his part in finding "suitable homes for orphans." He used *The Pleasure Boat* to match children with families willing to take them in. "If any honest faithful orphan, or other poor boy, either black or white, from twelve to fourteen years of age, will call on me, I will find a good home for him in a family, where he can do chores and attend school six or twelve months," Hacker announced; adding, "Any *bad* boy, who wishes to reform, shall have the same offer. Apply soon."¹⁰ Hacker also found homes for orphan girls. He tried to place siblings together.

The second solution Hacker proposed was to create a school to reform juveniles who had committed crimes. Hacker believed that jail did nothing to reform youngsters; rather, it had the opposite effect. "During their confinement," Hacker wrote, "they often occupy the same cells with the most abandoned men, and are exposed to the most obscene and filthy conversation and degrading habits. I have seen good looking boys not in their teens, playing cards with such characters, and the Jailor I am told, has no right to forbid it." Hacker had an idea for protecting young offenders: "If the city would prepare a farm on some one of its islands, in connection with a school and mechanical shop for such boys, many of them might be reformed." Hacker envisioned that the residential farm school would be a positive place, not a punitive one. There, the youth would learn an honest and healthy profession.¹¹

When Hacker proposed a farm school in 1847, nothing of the kind had been tried yet in Maine. But in Boston, reformers had been experimenting with the idea for some twenty years. The Boston House of Reformation for Juvenile Offenders was established in 1826 to reform and educate boys convicted of "petty crimes, vagrancy, and 'waywardness.'" The House of Reformation turned out to be more of a prison

---

9. *The Pleasure Boat*, June 23, 1845: 3.

10. *The Pleasure Boat*, June 23, 1845: 4.

11. *The Pleasure Boat*, Jan. 10, 1850: 2; Nov. 13, 1847: 4.

than a school. Under the leadership of its first superintendent, it had achieved some demonstrable success in reforming inmates, as less than twelve of the first 300 graduates reappeared in court for new offenses. However, the House of Reformation had long since deteriorated to become "a controversial, corrupt, often brutal custodial institution with a reputation as a school for crime from which many boys graduated to the State Prison."[12] In the meantime, a privately run Farm School had opened up on Boston's Thompson Island, which housed not juvenile offenders but simply "wayward youth" who had not been convicted of crimes. The school offered useful training "in practical occupation and Christian morals," to give disadvantaged boys a chance at a good, productive life.[13] It was to Boston's Farm School, not its House of Reform, that Hacker looked for inspiration. This became clear in 1850, after his idea began to gain acceptance, when he stated to his readers that he planned to visit the Boston Farm school "and collect all the information I can respecting that Institution."[14]

Hacker wanted a farm school so welcoming that juvenile offenders would choose to stay there rather than return to the streets. He claimed, "Give me the means to purchase an island and make it what it should be, and I would engage to make every bad boy in the city fall in love with it...."[15] Nay-sayers to Hacker's plan argued that this was impossible: juvenile offenders would not stay in such a school voluntarily and would have to be locked up. In order to prove them wrong, Hacker went into the jail one day in April of 1846 and bailed out three young offenders awaiting trial. He used his persuasive skills to get the jailor to lower the bail from $150 per child to $50 each. He then talked one of his loyal readers into paying the bail money, himself being a poor journalist. Hacker entrusted two of the boys to farmers he knew and one with

---

12. Peter C. Holloran, Boston's *Wayward Children: Social Services for Homeless Children 1830-1930* (Rutherford: Fairleigh Dickinson University Press, 1989), pp. 24-26.

13. Holloran, *Wayward Children*, 39.

14. *Portland Pleasure Boat*, Mar. 14, 1850: 3.

15. *Portland Pleasure Boat*, Mar. 14, 1850: 3.

the captain of a working boat. The goal was for them to learn a useful trade from a kind adult who cared for their well-being. None of the three boys ran away from their new homes. By the time they returned for their trials two months later, they were impressively reformed and honestly penitent, and their charges were dismissed. The scene in the courtroom was so moving that, according to Hacker, the judge and some of the lawyers wept.[16]

Hacker wrote this story serially as it was happening in his "Children's Cabin." It was a sort of parable for children, warning his young readers to be good themselves (so as not to end up in jail) and to be generous and compassionate to poor children. He recapped the story again in 1849, this time for adults. He printed extra copies of the story, and circulated it among members of the state legislature, the Portland city council, "and other influential men" to prove to them that kindness and education was better than punishment.[17] He continued writing on the subject regularly. Over the years, he further fleshed out his plan for the proposed reform school. It should consist of a farm, a trade school, and an academic school as well as a residence, all on a beautiful Casco Bay island. Residents of the school would be not only juvenile offenders but orphans. His reasoning was that orphans, having no home, would be glad for the clean, warm place to live, the chance at honest work, and the education. In addition, the orphans might be a good influence on those juveniles who had committed crimes. Hacker clearly meant the reform school to be all-male: for one thing, he never mentioned seeing girls in prison,[18] and Portland already had an orphan asylum for girls in

---

16. Summarized from the following accounts: *The Pleasure Boat*, Apr. 18, 1846: 3-4; June 27, 1846: 3-4; Aug. 23, 1849; *Chariot of Wisdom and Love*, July 13, 1865: 2.

17. *Chariot of Wisdom and Love*, July 13, 1865: 2.

18. This is not to suggest that there were no girls in jail; just that Hacker did not mention them. Women as well as men served time in jails. In the United States, women made up four to nineteen percent of the total prison population. A law passed in 1828 required that women and men be segregated in separate rooms.

Lucia Zedner, "Wayward Sisters: The Prison for Women," in *The Oxford History of the Prison*, ed. Norval Morris and David J. Rothman (Oxford: Oxford University Press, 1995), pp. 331-332.

the 1840s. With no orphanage in the city for boys, Hacker must have intended the residential reform school to fill this gap.

In February of 1850, Hacker gave cautionary support to the Portland City Council for appointing a committee "to devise the best means for punishing Juvenile offenders." Though Hacker was glad to hear that the city councilors were taking an interest in juvenile justice, he took issue with their choice of words. "Let them erase the word *punish* and place *reform, teach, save,* or some other word of sense in its place. How much better it would sound, to hear the Fathers talk of procuring a farm, establishing a school, &c., for saving by teaching orphans and other neglected children, than to talk about *punishing* them."[19] Hacker considered it an accomplishment when, in just two weeks, the newly formed committee decided in favor a reform school and prepared to petition the state Legislature.

State legislators were then flooded with petitions asking for a reform school. Impressed that such "influential and public spirited men" had signed these petitions, the Legislature voted in favor of the school. Governor John Hubbard signed the resolve on August 20, 1850. The Portland city government was given the task of selecting a site for the school. They found their perfect location, not on a Casco Bay island as Hacker had wanted, but in the rolling farmlands of Cape Elizabeth (which later became part of South Portland.) The city bought a 153-acre farm, and deeded it to the state of Maine on the condition "that the said estate shall always be held, used and forever improved by said State for such reform school." The State School for Boys, complete with a farm and a trade school, opened in 1853.[20]

The new school, of course, was not without problems. The boys who attended the school were locked into cells at night, which received minimal heating in the winter. Once the school was filled to capacity, its

---

19. *Portland Pleasure Boat*, Feb. 28, 1850: 3.

20. Edwin P. Wentworth, "Historical Sketch of the State School for Boys," in *Fiftieth Annual Report of the Trustees, Superintendent, Treasurer and Teachers of the State School for Boys, State of Maine, South Portland, December 1, 1903* (Augusta, ME: Kennebec Journal Print, 1904), pp. 50-l.

primitive facilities gave rise to disease. After the first death in 1855, the school was donated a plot at Forest City Cemetery.[21] The school was in actuality far different from the island home Hacker envisioned, which he had claimed "every bad boy in the city would fall in love with." It was essentially an age-segregated prison, albeit one where the inmates attended school and learned gardening and haying, among other useful skills. Hacker had nothing to do with the implementation of the reform school. Though he did keep himself and his readers informed on the school's progress, his main sources seemed to be the reports released by the school annually.[22] Hacker's humanitarian ideas did live on in writing, at least, if not in practice. In the forty-third annual report, written in 1897, the trustees of the State Reform school stated:

> The old, once prevailing opinion that boys are sent to a reform school to punish them, and that the buildings which constitute their homes are prisons... has long since been exploded. A reform school is an educational institution in its broadest sense. It involves not only the study of books, charts, maps, and other school appliances, but a physical, moral, industrial, and family training....[23]

Hacker would have been proud of these words.

It is difficult to determine how much Hacker and his writings actually effected concrete change. For example, we know that Hacker wrote about the need for a school, then Mainers petitioned the legislature, and the reform school was created. The events definitely happened in that order. But how much did the first fact affect the second and the third? To Hacker himself, the connection was clear. Years after the opening of the Reform School, he credited himself with the idea. He was offended that another journalist gave credit to Governor Hubbard,

---

21. Lionel G. Ouellette, *History of Southern Maine Juvenile Facility and Maine Youth Center* (South Portland, ME: Maine Youth Center's Graphic Arts Dept., 2000), pp. 4-5.

22. In 1858 Hacker mentioned receiving a trustee report, and concluding from it that the school "is doing an immense deal for the reform of juvenile offenders." *The Pleasure Boat*, Feb. 12, 1858: 4.

23. *Forty-Third Annual Report of the Trustees, Superintendent, Treasurer and Teachers of the State Reform School, State of Maine, South Portland, December 1, 1897* (Augusta: Kennebec Journal Print, 1897), p. 7.

who in fact implemented the plan. "The idea of the Reform School originated with the editor of the Pleasure Boat," Hacker insisted to readers in 1865, pointing out that no other Maine newspaper "except one, ever mentioned the subject until it came before the Legislature.... The School was a child of the Boat, and all that Gov. Hubbard ever did was to act as [midwife]...."[24]

---

24. *Chariot of Wisdom and Love*, July 13, 1865: 2.

Chapter 13

CONVERSATION ROOM: ANALYSIS OF HACKER'S IDEAS

Hacker's was a stern voice for freedom. He tried to convince others to be free from all superficial constraints—both great and small. He did this as an outsider and as someone who was himself seemingly free from the constraints he despised. As a person who practiced no organized religion, he asked people to leave their churches. As a man, he asked women to free themselves from constrictive fashion. As an abstainer from alcoholic beverage, he asked people to free themselves from addiction to alcohol. The only institution that he preached against that he himself was subject to was the government. Even though Hacker lived as a mostly law-abiding citizen and even petitioned the legislature at times, he tried to live his life as if there were no government. His success was mixed. He neither voted nor paid taxes. He used the court system sparingly, such as when he helped to free juvenile offenders. He did, however, use his press to publish laws passed by the state government.[1] And of course, the government service that was necessary to his trade was the postal service, without which he could not have spread his word effectively. Perhaps for that is why he gave it the affectionate nickname "Uncle Samuel."

The very facts that Hacker did petition the legislature, print state laws, and use the U.S. postal Service indicates potential flaws in his idea that people could live without government. It made sense in theory,

---

1. Hacker printed "Public Laws of the State of Maine, Passed by the Forty-fourth Legislature, A.D. 1865" as an Extra to *The Chariot of Wisdom and Love*, Jan. 25, 1865.

but did Hacker believe it would work in practice? Or was the end of government merely an unattainable goal he held out in front of himself and his loyal readers, as something to work toward? Hacker was not very specific about how to go about ending government. He obviously did not advocate an overthrow of the government; he wanted nothing so upsetting or violent. He seemed to think that the first step toward getting rid of the government was to convince people that they could be better off without it, which is what he essentially tried to do each week through his publication. He tried to free the minds of the people first in the hope that actual freedom would follow. If enough people ignored the government and lived their lives as though it did not exist (by refusing to vote, pay taxes, or use the court system, for example), the government would have no choice but to go away. People simply needed to prove they were worthy of independence and had no need for the laws, courts, and prisons the government provided them.

Hacker wrote: "My object has not been to reform the leaders—they are at present too intent on unrighteous gain—too earnest after the loaves and the fishes, to listen; they would only regard my testimony as the rattle of a pleasure boat. My work is with the people..."[2] Hacker's consistent message was that people should cast off their leaders, be they political or religious. He thought both types of leaders were equally stifling and that they were so intertwined that people needed to cast them both off together. Hacker felt that in order for people to live successfully without government, they would need excellent self-control and the ability to make the right moral decisions. Furthermore, the only way for people to have enough moral maturity to make the right decisions would be if they were free enough to have an individual relationship with God. Hacker's criticism of organized religions was that none of them allowed people to experience God individually. Hacker wrote that religious leaders used fear and bribery—the fear of God (or of the clergy) and the promise of heaven—to control people's actions "more

---

2. *The Pleasure Boat*, Oct. 20, 1845: 1.

firmly than they could by law."[3] So in order to be truly free and morally autonomous people, everyone had to rid themselves of controlling religious institutions.

Hacker believed that all of this could be brought about by persuasion, which explains why journalism was so important to him. He fervently believed that he knew the Truth and that when "honest seekers" heard it, they would recognize it as such. Perhaps he really believed that someday, people would live happily without poverty, crime, government, or institutions—religious or otherwise. Of course, he never saw that happen, even though he lived to see the passage of the Homestead Act. Although land was made available to Americans of all means and about two million Americans did take advantage of this,[4] poverty and crime did not go away. The need for government did not evaporate as Hacker had hoped. And yet, his vision of a world without government lived on in the anarchist movement, which was given voice in later years by the likes of Emma Goldman. And his vision of a world without religion lived on in the freethought movement, which Hacker helped inspire. When he died, *Free Thought Magazine* published a tribute to "Father Hacker, as he was called," declaring him to be "one of the 'saints' of the free thought movement."[5] To be considered a saint by a group of secular thinkers is a rare honor indeed.

As for his impact overall, Hacker might have been a more effective journalist had he not been so extreme. Had he been less inclined to attack ministers, politicians, and other trusted figures, he might not have been dismissed so easily by the mainstream public. Had he been more willing to compromise his vision of how the world should be, he might have had more influence through advising people on how to live

---

3. Jeremiah Hacker, *The Last Song of Jeremiah Hacker* (New Jersey: publisher not identified, 1893), p. 4.

4. According to the National Park Service, "some two million individuals" took advantage of the Homestead Act, which lasted from 1863 to 1976 in the lower orty-eight states, with a ten-year extension in Alaska. https://www.nps.gov/home/learn/historyculture/lasthomesteader.htm (Accessed February 10, 2018).

5. H. L. Greene, Ed. *Free Thought Magazine*, Vol. XIII, 1895: 740.

in the world as it was. He did, however, have moments of clarity during which he was able to take up causes that other people cared about too and speak to them in ways that they could hear. That was when Hacker was most effective. The people of Portland did not discount what they thought to be good sense when they heard it, even when it came from an extremist like Hacker. Hacker made the most sense to his fellow Portlanders when he attacked "quacks" like Dr. Carter, promoted land reform, and proposed a reform school for juvenile offenders.

In his book *American Reformers*, Ronald G. Walters points out the distinction between a reformer and a radical. Reformers work within the system to improve it. Their goal is not only to improve the lives of the needy, but to uphold the present order as well. A radical, on the other hand, works "to overturn the present order" and to "change the structure of society."[6] By these definitions, Hacker was by turns a reformer and a radical. When it came to his ideas on government and religion, he was certainly a radical. He had no interest in improving those institutions. He wanted to do away with them altogether. These turned out to be impossible goals because, as passionate as he was, he could not get the public to agree on what needed to be done.

There were times when Hacker was content to be a reformer, however, and worked within the system to improve problems one at a time, reaching solutions that, while not perfect, represented incremental improvements. His work with child welfare is one such example. Working within the existing social and political structure, Hacker was not only able to place several wayward children in homes, he also provided the impetus for the State School for Boys that is still in existence. Known now as the Long Creek Youth Development Center,[7] it is back in the

---

6. Walters, *American Reformers*, xxi.

7. The State School for Boys changed its name to The Maine Youth Center in 1976, when girls were first admitted to the facility. Recently, the name changed again to The Long Creek Youth Development Center. Still operated by the State of Maine, the center is located at the original site on Westbrook Street in South Portland. https://www.maine.gov/corrections/juvenile/Facilities/LCYDC/index.htm (Accessed February 10, 2018).

headlines as its future is debated.[8] But whatever its future, the old reform school that Hacker fought for so long ago was able to survive for more than a hundred years after his death.

---

8. The American Civil Liberties Union is calling for the facility's closure in favor of a "community-based model of juvenile justice." Eric Russell, "Long Creek's New Leader Concedes Juvenile Facility's at a Crossroads," *Portland Press Herald*, February 4, 2018, https://www.pressherald.com/2018/02/04/long-creeks-new-leader-concedes-juvenile-facilitys-at-a-crossroads/ (Accessed February 10, 2018).

Conclusion: Finding Hacker's Place in History

In 1928, a reporter from the *Portland Press Herald* obtained an 1850 copy of *The Pleasure Boat* and wrote a brief article about it. Calling the unconventional newspaper once printed in Portland a "unique temperance sheet," the *Press Herald* reporter concluded that the anonymous J. Hacker "did not mince words or spare anyone's feelings in the editorial columns" of his newspaper.[1] As it turns out, that was the last Portland heard of Hacker. The man who had spent his life writing had found no place in written history.

It is not completely surprising that Hacker was forgotten by history. He was too controversial to be remembered proudly or fondly, except by a small group of freethinkers who were inspired by his ideas, and despite the stir he created with tombstone epitaphs, he was not notorious enough to be remembered as a villain. He was simply a crank who had seemingly criticized nearly everyone and every cause at least once by the end of his long career. Portlanders in 1866 and Vinelanders in 1895 may have breathed a collective sigh of relief when Hacker was gone and may even have been happy to forget him. Hacker particularly did not endear himself to the makers or the writers of history. After all, he spoke out relentlessly against the government and other figures of authority. He spoke out against all of the wars that were fought in

---

1. "The Pleasure Boat Published in 1850, Didn't Mince Words." *Portland Sunday Telegram and Sunday Press Herald*, December 2, 1928: 13A.

his lifetime, regardless of their justifications or popularity. He railed against the increased industrialization that changed the landscape and economy of New England. In short, Hacker spoke out against what many people considered progress. As a result, his voice was drowned out in the dominant historical narrative.

It is interesting that Hacker complained about being left out of the history of the State School for Boys and that Governor Hubbard, a political leader, was given the credit for an idea that Hacker believed was his own. This should have come as no surprise to Hacker, since he must have known that much of what constitutes the historical narrative is politicized. By working outside the political realm, Hacker almost ensured his own historical anonymity. He was in the same boat (metaphorically speaking) as women, minorities, and other nineteenth-century groups that lacked political power. In her answer to the argument that women could do nothing to promote the cause of abolition, Maine activist Esther Gibbs said simply, "We can agitate."[2] Traditional history largely ignores the agitators who work for change outside the political arena, and Hacker was one of those. He was no politician, but he *was* an instigator. He wrote about the things he felt were wrong in society in the hope that if enough individuals cared, together their collective actions would bring about change. His method seemed to work sometimes, but even then, it is hard to prove how much impact Hacker as agitator actually had on the outcome.

Why wasn't Hacker remembered for his writing alone? William Lloyd Garrison, editor of *The Liberator* in Boston, has a respected place in New England history for his role as a journalist. But Garrison, a contemporary of Hacker's, was much better known in his lifetime as a lecturer and organizer. Today, Garrison is mostly remembered within the context of the cause he worked for: the abolition of slavery. Hacker had no such strong associations. He was too independent to speak for

---

2. Edward O. Schriver, *Go Free: The Antislavery Impulse in Maine, 1833-1855* (Orono, ME: University of Maine Press, 1970), pp. 37, 44.

any movements beyond himself. As one of his contemporaries put it, Hacker's newspaper was "devoted to Hackerism."[3]

In any case, Hacker has been largely forgotten. He is not quoted in history textbooks. His articles do not appear in anthologies. If you want to read Hacker's words today, you have to wear white gloves. The densely-printed three-column pages of *The Pleasure Boat* are bound together in fragile volumes that are kept in glass cases in the back rooms of libraries. How they got there is a story in itself. With the help of "Uncle Samuel," Hacker mailed his *Boats* and *Chariots* to far-flung subscribers each week, so he knew how far his ideas were distributed. As he told one little girl who had written a letter into the *Chariot*,

> Do you know how far your letter will go in the Chariot? I guess not, so I will tell you. It will go to New Brunswick and Nova Scotia, to Canada and California, and a few copies will go to England and Scotland. It will be read by more boys and girls than you ever saw in all your little seven years of life.[4]

As he spread his ideas far and wide, Hacker also worked to ensure that they would outlast him. He asked his loyal readers to save their newspapers for their children. He offered to send subscribers missing issues for free, so they could have complete sets. He passed on information about bookbinders he knew who could be hired to bind a volume of newspapers in leather for a reasonable fee. Readers around the country and around the world followed Hacker's advice and, thanks to them, volumes of *The Pleasure Boat* and *The Chariot of Wisdom and Love* made their way to libraries, universities, and historical societies, not only in Maine and the maritime provinces of Canada, but in Massachusetts, New York, Virginia, Iowa, Wisconsin, Michigan, Kansas, Texas, New Mexico, California, Washington, Alberta, and British Columbia. Although none of them wound up in England or Scotland, some *Boats* drifted

---

3. *Portland Pleasure Boat*, October 16, 1851: 4.

4. *Chariot of Wisdom and Love*, Sept. 1865: 7.

over the North Sea and landed in Germany.[5] This gives an idea of the geographic distribution of Hacker's readers, and how widespread this small community of reformers was.

Although Hacker did not secure a place for himself in written history, his words remain to be excavated by curious students and local historians, due to these individual acts of preservation. Today, his writings not only give insight into his character, but also illuminate other partly buried histories. Hacker provides a fascinating first-hand account, for example, of the Second Great Awakening in Maine. He describes the fervor and strong emotions he witnessed and inspired, and groups he encountered, such as the Millerites in Litchfield. As a disaffected Quaker, Hacker offers the perspective of someone who felt alienated by the changes brought about by the Wilberite-Gurneyite division in the 1840s. His writings on this subject help shed light on the overall Quaker experience in Maine at the time. As a reformer, Hacker lets us glimpse the lives of the poor and powerless in Portland, humanizing the individuals who might otherwise just be names on a census record, if any trace remains at all. As an early anarchist and freethinker, Hacker broadens our understanding of these movements that have, like him, been largely ignored by history. Finally, and perhaps most importantly, Hacker's strong voice of dissent reminds us that even though history happened in the way it did, some people cried out against what was happening. He was an articulate witness to his times, even while making clear that he wished his times were different.

Rediscovered through his writings, Hacker takes on personality and becomes a historical figure in his own right. We can picture him teaching penmanship, preaching in town halls and on the roadside, visiting prisoners in the county jail, selling newspapers on the streets of Portland, and listening to complaints through an ear trumpet. We can picture him

---

5. Many of these are listed in Winifred Gregory's *Union List of Serials in Libraries of the United States and Canada,* Second edition, (New York: H. W. Wilson, 1943), p. 2242. Also, an OCLC WorldCat search for "Pleasure Boat" turns up more locations, https://www.worldcat.org/title/hackers-pleasure-boat/oclc/809138269?referer=di&ht=edition (accessed March 3, 2018).

growing sweet potatoes, writing infidel poems, and drawing a crowd in the public square as an old man in New Jersey. Jeremiah Hacker deserves at least a small place in history as a homegrown New England radical, an independent journalist, a champion of free speech, a prison reformer, an abolitionist, a pacifist, a free land advocate, an anarchist, a "saint" of the freethought movement, and an unrelenting voice of dissent.

BIBLIOGRAPHY

Primary Sources

1850 Census, Portland, Maine. Roll 252, National Archives Microfilm Publications, 1934.

1860 Census, Brunswick, Maine. Series M653, Roll 437, http://heritagequestonline.com.

1860 Census, Westbrook, Maine. Series M653, Roll 436, p. 35, http://heritagequestonline.com.

1880 United States Federal Census, Berlin, Camden, New Jersey; Roll: 775; Page: 615D; Enumeration District: *066.* Ancestry.com and The Church of Jesus Christ of Latter-day Saints.

Barry, William David. *Maine: The Wilder Half of New England.* Gardiner, ME: Tillbury House Publishers, 2012.

Beckett, S. B. *The Portland Directory.* Portland, ME: Thurston & Co.,1846, 1847, 1852, 1856, 1858, 1863, and 1866.

Chase, Warren. *Forty Years on the Spiritualist Rostrum.* Boston: Colby & Rich Publishers, 1888.

Child, Henry Teas. "Spiritualism in Pennsylvania. Official Report of the Seventh Annual Meeting of the Pennsylvania Society of Spiritualists, H eld at Institute Hall, Philadelphia, April 1st, 1873." *Religio-Philosophical Journal,* May 10, 1873. http://www.iapsop.com/spirithistory/pennsylvania_society_of_spiritualists.html.

The Daily True American. Trenton, NJ: Morris R. Hamilton, 1895.

Dow, Neal. *The Reminiscences of Neal Dow: Recollections of Eighty Years*. Portland, ME: The Evening Express Publishing Company, 1898.

Eastern Argus. Portland, ME: I. Berry & Co., 1818–1846.

The Firebrand. Ed. Abe Isaak, Henry Addis, and Abner J. Pope. Portland, OR: Firebrand Publishing, 1895-1897.

Forty-Third Annual Report of the Trustees, Superintendent, Treasurer and Teachers of the State Reform School. Augusta, ME: Kennebec Journal Print, 1897.

Goldman, Emma. "Anarchism: What It Really Stands For" (1911). Reprinted in *The Radical Reader*, edited by Timothy Patrick McCarthy and John McMillian, 288-95. New York: The New Press, 2003.

Greene, H. L., ed. *The Free Thought Magazine*, Vol. 13. Chicago: H. L. Greene, 1895.

Hacker, Jeremiah. *The Chariot of Wisdom and Love*. Portland, ME: Jeremiah Hacker, 1864-1866.

———. *Hacker's Pleasure Boat*. Berlin, NJ: Jeremiah Hacker, 1867-1888.

———. "Journal of Jeremiah Hacker." *The Vineland Historical Magazine* 17 no. 4-19 no. 1. Vineland, NJ: Vineland Historical and Antiquarian Society, 1932-1934.

———. *The Last Song of Jeremiah Hacker, Now of Vineland, New Jersey*. New Jersey: publisher not identified, 1893.

———. *A Lecture*. Berlin, N.J.: s.n., 1886.

———. *The Pleasure Boat*. Portland, ME: Jeremiah Hacker, 1845-1847.

———. *The Portland Pleasure Boat*. Portland, ME: Jeremiah Hacker, 1847-1862.

Harris, Harlowe. *Portland Directory*. Portland, ME: Arthur Shirley & Son, 1841.

Bibliography

Hall, Rufus. "From a letter written to Rufus Hacker Hall and Anna Hoag from their son Rufus." http://hatevilhalls.org/Halls.org/LETTERS%20THAT%20WERE%20WRITTEN.html.

Holden, Charles. "The Origin and History of the Newspaper Press in Cumberland County." *Transactions of the Editors and Publishers' Association of Maine, August 4th and 5th, 1869*. Portland, ME: Monitor Printing, 1869.

Kelley, Judith Holbrook, ed. *Marriage Returns of Cumberland County, Maine, Prior to 1898*. Rockport, ME: Picton Press, 1998.

Kennedy, Hon. J. C. G. *Catalogue of the Newspapers and Periodicals Published in the United States*. New York: John Livingston, 1852.

Lord, John P. *The Maine Townsman, or Laws for the Regulation of Towns: with Forms and Judicial Decisions, Adapted to the Revised Statutes of Maine*. Portland, ME: Sanborn & Carter, 1847.

Lucifer the Light-Bearer. Ed. Moses Harman, Lillian Harman, and Edwin C. Walker. Valley Falls, KS, Topeka, KS, and Chicago IL, 1883-1907

Neal, John. "The Pleasure Boat," *Portland Transcript*. Portland, ME: s.n., 1848.

———. *Wandering Recollections of a Somewhat Busy Life. An Autobiography*. Boston: Roberts Brothers, 1869.

"Pine Grove Cemetery." *Brunswick Area Cemetery Records*. Brunswick, ME: Pejepscot Historical Society, n.d.

"The Pleasure Boat Published in 1850, Didn't Mince Words." *Portland Sunday Telegram and Sunday Press Herald*, December 2, 1928: 13A.

Portland Advertiser. Portland, ME: Gerrish & Edwards, 1847.

The Portland Directory. Portland, ME: Arthur Shirley, 1834 and 1837.

Portland Transcript. Portland, ME: s.n., 1895.

Putnam, Henry. *A Description of Brunswick, (Maine;) in Letters by a Gentleman from South Carolina, to a Friend in that State*. Brunswick: Joseph Griffin, 1820.

Varney, George J. *A Gazetteer of the State of Maine.* Boston: B. B. Russell, 1886.

Wheeler, George Augustus, M.D., and Henry Warren Wheeler. *History of Brunswick, Topsham, and Harpswell, Maine.* Boston: Alfred Mudge & Sons, 1878.

The Wichita Daily Eagle. Whichita, KS: M.M. Murdock & R.P. Murdock, 1895.

Secondary Sources

"Amelia Bloomer," *Encyclopaedia Britannica.* Encyclopaedia Britannica, Inc., 2017. https://www.britannica.com/biography/Amelia-Bloomerhttps://www.britannica.com/biography/Amelia-Bloomer.

Bacon, Margaret Hope. *The Quiet Rebels: The Story of Quakers in America.* Philadelphia: New Society Publishers, 1985.

Barry, William David, and Nan Cumming. *Rum, Riot and Reform: Maine and the History of American Drinking.* Portland, ME: Impressive Printing, 1998.

Blumin, Stuart M. "Introduction: George G. Foster and the Emerging Metropolis." In *New York by Gas-Light and Other Urban Sketches* by George G. Foster, 27-35. Berkeley: University of California Press, 1990.

Bowden, Martyn J. "Mercantile Portland." In *Historical Atlas of Maine*, edited by Stephen J. Hornsby and Richard W. Judd, plate 36. Orono, ME: The University of Maine Press, 2015.

Braude, Ann. *Radical Spirits: Spiritualism and Women's Rights in Nineteenth-Century America.* Bloomington: Indiana University Press, 2001.

Brock, Peter. *Pacifism in the United States, From the Colonial Era to the First World War.* Princeton, NJ: Princeton University Press, 1968.

Brunelle, Jim. *Maine Almanac.* Portland, ME: Guy Gannett Publishing, 1978.

Comfort, William Wistar. *The Quaker Persuasion Yesterday, Today, Tomorrow.* Philadelphia: Frederick H. Gloeckner, 1956.

Cooper, Robert Alan. "The English Quakers and Prison Reform 1809-23." *Quaker History* 68, no. 1 (1979): 3-19

Curti, Merle. Peace or War: The American Struggle, 1636-1936. Boston: J. S. Cranner & Co., 1959.

Dean, Walter. "The Lost Meaning of 'Objectivity.'" *American Press Institute*. https://www.americanpressinstitute.org/journalism-essentials/bias-objectivitiy/lost-meaning-objectivity/.

"Dorothea Dix Begins Her Crusade," MassMoments, Mass Humanities, https://www.massmoments.org/moment-details/dorothea-dix-begins-her-crusade.html

Eastman, Joel W. and Paul E. Rivard. "Transportation and Manufacturing." In *Maine: The Pine Tree State from Prehistory to the Present*, edited by Richard A. Judd et al., 310-69. Orono, ME: University of Maine Press: 1995.

Erikson, Patricia. "Deconstructing the Vanishing American Paradigm: Native Americans and the Next Generation of Anthropology." Amherst, MA: University of Massachusetts, 1998. http://www.umass.edu/legal/derrico/erikson.html.

Friends of Historic Vineland, "A Ticket to Vineland—The Adult Version." http://www.vineland.org/history/friends/ticket/html.

Grammer, Elizabeth Elkin. *Some Wild Visions: Autobiographies by Female Itinerant Evangelists in Nineteenth-Century America*. Oxford: Oxford University Press, 2003.

Gregory, Winifred, ed. *Union List of Serials in Libraries of the United States and Canada*. 2nd ed. New York: The H. W. Wilson Co., 1943.

Griffin, Joseph, ed. *History of the Press in Maine*. Brunswick, ME: From the Press, 1919.

Guarneri, Carl J. "George Henry Evans." In *American National Biography*, 603-4. Oxford: Oxford University Press, 1999.

Holloran, Peter C. *Boston's Wayward Children: Social Services for Homeless Children 1830-1930*. Rutherford, NJ: Fairleigh Dickinson University Press, 1989.

Hornsby, Stephen J. and Wayne M. O'Leary. "Maritime Trade." In *Historical Atlas of Maine*, edited by Stephen J. Hornsby and Richard W. Judd, plate 34. Orono, ME: The University of Maine Press, 2015.

Jacoby, Susan. *Freethinkers: A History of American Secularism*. New York: Metropolitan Books, 2004.

Jordan, William B. *Index to Portland Newspapers, 1785-1835*. Bowie, MD: Heritage Books, 1994.

Kurlansky, Mark. *Cod: A Biography of the Fish that Changed the World*. New York: Penguin Books, 1997.

McCarthy, Timothy Patrick and John McMillan, eds. *The Radical Reader: A Documentary History of the American Radical Tradition*. New York: The New Press, 2003.

McElroy, Wendy. "The Free-Soil Movement." *Freedom Daily*, May 2001. http://www.troynovant.com/McElroy/Essays/Free-Soil-Movement.html.

McMullen, Ann. "What's Wrong with This Picture? Context, Conversion, Survival and the Development of Regional Native Cultures and Pan-Indianism in Southeastern New England." In *Enduring Traditions: The Native Peoples of New England*, edited by Laurie Weinstein, 123-50. Westport, CT: Bergin & Garvey, 1994.

Meagher, Paul Kevin et al., eds. *Encyclopedic Dictionary of Religion*. Vol. 1 of 3. Washington, D.C.: Corpus Publications, 1979.

National Park Service. "The Last Homesteader." Homestead National Monument of America. https://www.nps.gov/home/learn/historyculture/lasthomesteader.htm.

New England Yearly Meeting. *Faith and Practice of New England Yearly Meeting of Friends*. Worcester, MA: New England Yearly Meeting of Friends, 1985.

Noll, Mark A. *America's God: From Jonathan Edwards to Abraham Lincoln*. Oxford: Oxford University Press, 2002.

Norton, Mary Beth et al. *A People and a Nation*. Vol. 1 of 2. Boston: Houghton Mifflin, 1994.

Oickle, Alvin F. *Jonathan Walker the Man with the Branded Hand.* Everett, MA: Lorelli Slater Publisher, 1998.

Ouellette, Lionel G. *History of Southern Maine Juvenile Facility and Maine Youth Center.* South Portland, ME: Maine Youth Center Graphic Arts Department, 2000.

"Recollections of Joel and Huldah Heacock," http://www.starwarsfan.freeservers.com/RECOLLECTIONS.htm.

Roberts, Nancy L. "The Peace Advocacy Press." In *Outsiders in Nineteenth-Century Press History: Multicultural Perspectives*, edtied by Frankie Hutton and Barbara Strauss Reed, 209-38. Bowling Green, OH: Bowling Green State University Popular Press, 1995.

Russell, Eric. "Long Creek's New Leader Concedes Juvenile Facility's at a Crossroads." *Portland Press Herald*, February 4, 2018. https://www.pressherald.com/2018/02/04/long-creeks-new-leader-concedes-juvenile-facilitys-at-a-crossroads/.

Senior, Donald, ed. *The Catholic Study Bible: The New American Bible.* Oxford: Oxford University Press, 1990.

Schriver, Edward O. and Stanley R. Howe. "The Republican Ascendancy: Politics and Reform." In *Maine: The Pine Tree State from Prehistory to the Present*, edited by Richard A. Judd et al., 370-90. Orono, ME: University of Maine Press, 1995.

Shettleworth, Earle G. Jr., and William David Barry. *Mr. Goodhue Remembers Portland: Scenes from the Mid-Nineteenth Century.* Augusta, ME: Maine Historic Preservation Commission, 1981.

Shi, David E. *The Simple Life: Plain Living and High Thinking in American Culture.* Oxford: Oxford University Press, 1985.

Sim, John L. *The Grassroots Press: America's Community Newspapers.* Ames, IA: Iowa University Press, 1969.

Smith, Melanie B. "Pews for Sale, for Rent." *The Decatur Daily*, September 11, 2004. http://www.decaturdaily.com/decaturdaily/religion.040911/sale.html.

State of Maine Department of Corrections. "Long Creek Youth Development Center." http://www.maine.gov/corrections/juvenile/Facilities/LCYDC/index.htm.

Stattler, Richard D. *Guide to the Records of the Religious Society of Friends (Quakers) in New England*. Providence, RI: Rhode Island Historical Society, 1997.

Stephenson, George M. *The Puritan Heritage*. New York: Macmillan, 1952.

Streeter, Donald. "Bibliographical Sketch [of Jeremiah Hacker]." *The Vineland Historical Magazine* 17 no. 4 (1932): 204-5.

Summers, Lydia B., ed. *Portland*. Portland, ME: Greater Portland Landmarks, 1999.

Walters, Ronald G. *American Reformers 1815-1860*. New York: Hill & Wang, 1978.

Weeks, Silas B. *New England Quaker Meetinghouses Past and Present*. Richmond, IN: Friends United Press, 2001.

Wentworth, Edwin P. "Historical Sketch of the State School for Boys." In *Fiftieth Annual Report of the Trustees, Superintendent, Treasurer, and Teachers of the State School for Boys*, 48-58. Augusta, ME: Kennebec Journal Print, 1904.

Wright, Luella M. *The Literary Life of Early Friends*. New York: AMS Press, 1966.

Zedner, Lucia. "Wayward Sisters: The Prison for Women." In *The Oxford History of the Prison*, edited by Norval Morris and David J. Rothman. Oxford: Oxford University Press, 1995.

Zinn, Howard. *A People's History of the United States*. New York: Perennial Classics, 2001.

About the Author

Rebecca M. Pritchard studied writing at the Salt Institute in Portland, Maine, and American & New England Studies at the University of Southern Maine. In school, she became interested in the stories buried in old newspapers and spent her time in libraries poring over their wrinkled pages. She has worked for the Maine Historical Society, the Abbe Museum, and Acadia National Park. She lives with her husband and daughter in Bar Harbor, Maine where she writes for *The Mount Desert Islander*. *Jeremiah Hacker: Journalist, Anarchist, Abolitionist* is her first book.

www.ingramcontent.com/pod-product-compliance
Lightning Source LLC
Chambersburg PA
CBHW052051070526
44584CB00017B/2131